THE
PUBLICATIONS
OF THE
THORESBY SOCIETY

ESTABLISHED IN THE YEAR

MDCCCLXXXIX

SECOND SERIES

VOLUME 17

FOR 2006

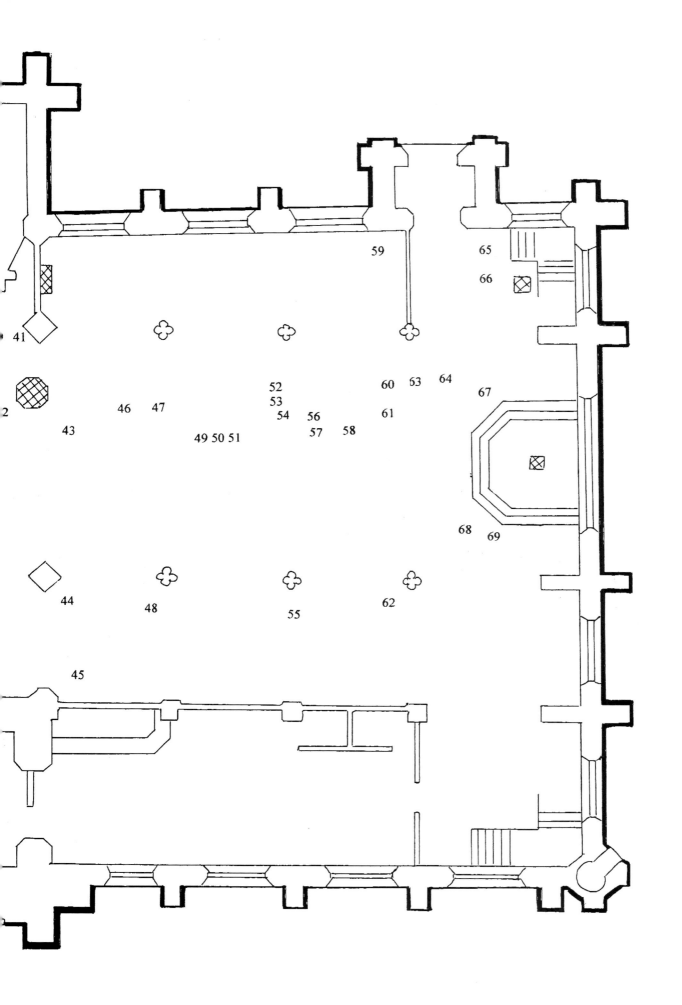

PREFACE

THE PARISH CHURCH of St Peter-at-Leeds contains hundreds of monuments. Many are placed in relatively inaccessible places, either high on the walls or partially obscured by furniture and fittings; a number are so worn or damaged they are difficult to read. In consequence, casual visitors to the church would find it challenging to decipher the inscriptions surrounding them. Even those visitors determined to find a monument dedicated to a particular group or person may well decide after a while to give up the attempt.

Presenting the monuments in a manner that is logical and easily followed has been a challenge and one that I fear can never be entirely satisfactorily resolved. I have made an attempt, however, and this book has been designed so that those who wish to visit the church and view the monuments *in situ* may use it as an aid. The monuments are listed in order as they appear on the walls or floors, which in many cases will be out of context with reference to other family members or groups. Though many of the monuments were rescued from the medieval church during demolition and placed in the present church, their replacement was often haphazard. Further changes have occurred in the intervening years and are to continue, so this book must necessarily reflect the parish church as it appears at the time of writing.

For the purposes of this study I have divided the church into discrete areas and listed the monuments appearing in each area as a group before moving to the next. I hope this will allow the visitor to move around the church in a logical sequence. This approach means, of course, that the monuments do not appear in any sort of chronological order; they appear as they do in the church itself, an interesting and random mix. For the mural monuments I have adapted the convention used by the NADFAS Church Recorders, in that the east window (or equivalent) of each area is taken as the starting point and the monuments follow round the points of the compass from there. The highest-placed monument to the right of the east window is number one, the one below is number two, etc. The movement is always top to bottom and left to right. In the same way, the various areas within the church have been dealt with similarly, moving left to right from the east window to the sanctuary, the south aisle, west end and north aisle. The side chapels, north tower and gallery are dealt with in the same fashion.

The floor slabs presented a different challenge. Most of the slabs have been placed so the inscriptions are read with one's back to the altar and again the decision was taken to number them in sequence, from left to right as read, row by row, within their discrete areas. Thus the first floor slab on the altar flats is that nearest the east end and by the south wall, number two is next to it on the right and so on. When that row was completed the next row started again with the slab nearest the south wall, one row back.

Each of the monuments has been identified according to location and given an individual number reflecting the sequence. The prefix Wa.T. indicates a wall or mural tablet; M.S. identifies a monument slab or floor slab. The freestanding effigy has simply been identified as such and the two table monuments are described similarly as Table Monuments. Inevitably, it is confusing and I can only apologise and assure the reader that I have spent many hours feeling puzzled and lost myself.

For those readers interested in particular individuals rather than the church as a whole I have included an index whereby everyone mentioned by name on a monument is listed temporary, not only just remaining to bedevil the historian. In parish registers it is common to see the month of January notated, for example, as 1734/5, even though the date at March 25 would be given as 1735. A date shown as 1 February 1709/10 would therefore signify February 1710 New Style.

The easy temptation to simply write the date as the 1 February 1710 should be resisted, as the actual day would be different by eleven days from our modern reckoning. For our purposes it is correctly given as 1 February 1709/10, which clearly indicates it belongs to the Julian Calendar.

A careless reading of dates could result in entirely erroneous assumptions. For example, in the Lady Chapel of Leeds Parish Church, a brass[29] commemorates the two young sons of Alderman Marmaduke Hicke: 'William who dyed December the 25th 1673' and 'Iohn their elder sonne who dyed Iannuary the 7th 1673'. On first reading it would appear the two children died within eleven months of each other, with John, although commemorated second on the memorial, dying first. In the *Parish Register of Burials*,[30] however, the boys are recorded thus: 'William, son of Mr Marmaduke Hick Alderman, of ye Borelaine' who was buried 27 December 1673 and 'John, son of Mr Marmaduke Hick Alderman, of ye: Borelaine' buried 9 January 1673/4. They therefore died within a fortnight of each other possibly both from an infectious disease. It also perhaps alters our perception of their surviving family: to lose two young children in the space of a few days would be a terrible tragedy even in those times of high infant mortality.

Textual notes accompanying the memorial transcriptions warn where the dates in the epitaphs could cause confusion, with corroboration from contemporary sources, generally entries in the parish registers or newspapers. Entries in the index also try to clarify ambiguities, with the year of John Hicke's death for example, given as 1673/4.

EARLY LEEDS[31]

Archaeological finds dating from the Bronze Age have been found scattered throughout Leeds and two barrows on Woodhouse Moor were excavated in the nineteenth century. Earthworks nearby, by Rampart Road, may have represented an Iron Age fort, and Roman material and the remains of a Roman road have also been uncovered. Leeds, as reference by Bede suggests,[32] was probably a major Anglo-Saxon settlement. That it was indeed a major religious centre is corroborated by the discovery of fragments of at least six Anglo-Saxon crosses, the best preserved of which is in the parish church.

Leeds seems somehow to have escaped the Harrying of the North, which followed the Norman Conquest. By 1086, according to the Domesday Book, it possessed a priest, a church, a mill and meadowland.[33]

In 1207 the Borough Charter given by Maurice Paynel, the lord of the manor, created a new town: a small borough within the bounds of the manor.[34] A stone bridge across the Aire existed by at least 1322 and the new street of Briggate was laid out from the river north to Kirkgate with thirty plots on either side and the space for a market. The charter encouraged crafts and trade and by the fifteenth century cloth-making was firmly established in the town.[35] Until the seventeenth century, however, Leeds remained small and essentially rural in character.

THE MERCANTILE COMMUNITY OF
LEEDS SEVENTEENTH – TWENTIETH
CENTURIES

It was during the seventeenth century that Leeds effected the transformation from a small market town to a commercial, manufacturing and distribution centre, which took influence and business away from the thitherto principal regional towns, York and Halifax. The Charter of Incorporation of 1626 created a free borough with a self-elected governing Corporation, possessing the power to issue by-laws, appoint local officers and to regulate, inspect and control the cloth produced in the town.[36] In 1629 the Corporation, led by Richard Sykes, bought the manor of Leeds from the Crown.[37]

The sympathies of the population of Leeds were divided by the Civil War, with the mercantile class generally remaining loyal to the King and the clothiers declaring their support for Parliament.[38] The town was besieged in January 1642/3,[39] and was eventually taken by General Sir Thomas Fairfax, a cousin of the Thomas Fairfax commemorated in the parish church. Reminders of the Civil War in the parish church include the monument slab to Garvas Neville, whose epitaph recorded that he was the Quartermaster General for the Marquis of Newcastle.[40] The merchant, John Thoresby, represents the Parliamentarians: he distinguished himself at the battle of Marston Moor.[41]

During the Restoration the town flourished and Leeds rapidly became a centre of importance in the cloth trade. Cloth from villages to the south and west was brought into the town for dressing, cropping and dyeing and the finished cloth was marketed by a wealthy group of merchants.[42] From Leeds, the woollen cloth was sent to Hull and thence to markets in Holland and Germany, where the merchants had agents. Alliances were built up amongst the great mercantile families who governed the town and ran its affairs, forming a ruling oligarchy. They intermarried and the same names, Kitchingman, Fenton, Lodge, Milner, Cookson, and Ibbetson among them, appear and reappear time and again over the years.[43]

These were men of immense wealth and influence. Some were exceptionally far-sighted businessmen, well able to exploit opportunities as they presented themselves. William Milner, for example, was one of the prime promoters during his mayoralty of the Aire and Calder Navigation, the waterway that made the rivers Aire and Calder navigable. Work on cutting the canal to improve the rivers was initially undertaken in 1699–1701 and for the first twenty years of its existence Milner managed the affairs of its ruling company so that by 1720 he had raised £26,700 in dues from the local merchant community.[44] Fabulously wealthy, he was a friend of Lord Irwin (and often lent him money) ran racehorses, had townhouses in London and York and spent huge sums promoting buildings and improvements in Leeds.[45]

In those early days the merchants generally still had their feet very firmly on the ground. Their house plots in the town incorporated yards, outbuildings and offices[46] and their sons were given every encouragement to follow in the family business. Apprenticeships lasted four to seven years commencing at about the age of fifteen. The apprentice lived with his master's family, went daily to the counting house and finishing shops and regularly visited the cloth markets of Leeds, Wakefield and Halifax. He was indentured and obliged to keep industrious, to mind his master's business, keep out of trouble and shun dubious company.[47] Often he spent a year abroad to visit foreign correspondents and learn languages, particularly French, Dutch and German. James Ibbetson and William Milner both spent several years in Holland in the 1690s;[48] Ralph Thoresby was sent to Holland in 1678 after an initial year's training in London, but was recalled after only six months due to his father's sudden death.[49] Business contacts with the continent flourished, and several foreigners came speculatively to Leeds to join existing merchant houses or to set up business there on their own account: Koster and Bischoff among them.[50]

With increasing prosperity, however, some of the early families had ambitions beyond trade and toward gentrification. William Milner sent his son to Eton and Jesus College Cambridge[51] and in the early eighteenth century James Ibbetson sent his elder son to the Inns of Court.[52] Both men had ambitions for their sons beyond mere trade. Milner bought the estate of Nun Appleton and Bolton Percy near York in 1711 and the Ibbetsons purchased the old Fairfax estate at Denton, near Ilkley, where John Carr of York was commissioned to build a magnificent country mansion.[53] Thus, as the years passed the old family firms gradually disappeared.[54]

Meanwhile, vigorous newcomers entered the business community and essentially followed the same pattern: in 1764 Arthur Lupton went to Frankfurt upon Main to learn High Dutch, French and accounts,[55] and Henry Hall was in Delph c. 1790 to learn Dutch and French.[56] Generally only the sons not going into the business were educated for the professions. Training the son chosen to continue the family business required a substantial sum of money to be devoted to a long apprenticeship. Indeed, there were complaints about the exorbitant rates charged by the local merchants before they would agree to take on a young man as an apprentice.[57]

Business concerns dominated most, if not all, aspects of the lives of the merchants. Marriages tended to be dynastic: they were made with an eye to matrimonial settlements which brought money into the family and to the business. If necessary the wife's portion could be used to aid the business through difficulties and marriage settlements were an important source of business finance. By 1750 an aspiring merchant would seek a wife who could provide a dowry of at least £1000.[58] This was a wholly accepted part of an alliance. By the mid-eighteenth century it was commonplace for the wealth a bride brought to her husband to be announced as a matter of congratulation in the local newspapers: 'Yesterday was married at our Parish Church, Mr. William Wilson … to Miss Pawson, an agreeable Lady, with a Fortune of 20,000 *l*.';[59] 'Last week, Henry Ibbetson, Esq: was married to Miss Carr, eldest Daughter of Ralph Carr, Esq: of Durham, a beautiful young lady of good Fortune …';[60] James Kenion 'an eminent Apothecary in this Town, to Miss Parkinson of Hatfield nigh Doncaster, an agreeable young Lady with a considerable Fortune';[61] 'Yesterday was married at our Parish Church, Mr Francis Ridsdale, Merchant, to Miss Green, Daughter to Mr. Joseph Green of This Town, a Lady of great

Bartholomew Ibbetson (died 1676) and Guglielmus Horne (died 1685). Of these supplemental memorials, the plaques for Ibbetson and Horne have survived. Ibbetson's has been moved to the nave and Horne's is now found on a window sill in the Lady Chapel. By Thoresby's time, the slab containing Thomas Clarell's memorial also carried a commemorative brass for John Thwaites (died 1671). Thwaites's was subsequently removed from its medieval ground to a Lady Chapel window sill.[167]

Thoresby's strictures over the lack of respect and care that the older monuments had been afforded over the years strongly suggests that there had been few scruples over the re-use of stones. A re-use and modernizing of the older monuments could explain the anomalous context of the remaining Egglestone marble slabs in the church; despite the virtual cessation of production by the quarries after the Reformation, most of the Egglestone marble monuments in the parish church carry inscriptions of a conspicuously later date. The monument for John Douglas and his family, for example, covers the dates 1621 to 1765. In the *Ducatus* it is described as 'a new marble' and the dates thereon range from 1621 to 1699.[168]

Most of the Egglestone marble slabs in the church, furthermore, commemorate burials from the eighteenth century. The dates on Jeremiah Barstow's slab range from 1711 to 1719; those on Elizabeth Fenton's slab range from 1714 to 1777. Catharine Ibbetson's death occurred in 1740 and the inscription also commemorates the death of her husband, Sir Henry, in 1761. John Firth's slab has an inscription covering the years 1741 to 1755; William Cookson's carries dates from 1743 to 1811; Thomas Bywater's from 1762 to 1824; and Henry Hall's from 1796 to 1805. Harriott Mason died in 1798 and the slab for Harrison Owler is too worn for a date to be deciphered.

Virtually all of these post-medieval inscriptions have worn very badly and are thus difficult to read. In contrast to the deep-set indents remaining on the medieval monuments, the later inscribed letters almost appear to be scratched on the surface. Certainly, the later Egglestone marble monuments have survived far less well than contemporary ones cut into the more prevalent dark limestone monument slabs elsewhere in the church.

In all, Thoresby described ten slabs that could have been medieval in origin. In addition to the Clarell and Langton memorials he noted seven other stones which cannot now be identified. Of one he wrote: 'upon another ancient Marble, the Brass whereof is inhumanly torn off are these modern Inscriptions' which range from 1674 to 1706. None of these inscriptions survive. Of another he wrote: 'The next marble seems to be Ancient, yet has no Inscriptions save for Mr. James Lobley of Hunslet-Lane, 25 Aug. 1661…'. This stone is also lost as are the following: 'The ancient Inscription and Arms in Brass inlaid upon the Adjacent Marble are barbarously torn off. The modern is for Henry, Son of Stephen Eamondson 5 Apr. 1659 … The next Stone has had the same Fate. What remains are for Isabel, pious Wife of Henry Eadmondson, 17 May 1674.' … 'Upon an ancient Marble – Hannah wife of Mr Barth Towers of Leedes … 1678' … 'In the South Quire two ancient Marbles curiously inlaid with Brass, one in the Form of an Antique Cross, the other 2 Statues and 4 Plates of Brass all with the Inscriptions most barbarously torn off, Upon the former is now a modern Brass [Thomas Barnard, died 1685] …Upon the other Marble, Elizabeth, wife of Ed. Bolton, 1619.'[169]

It cannot be determined, of course, whether the missing stones described by Thoresby were Egglestone marble. Plainly, a number of medieval monument slabs have been lost since his survey and the ancient monuments generally were not treated as artifacts intrinsically deserving of respect but were re-used and added to as deemed necessary, particularly from the seventeenth century onwards. Indeed, the turmoil and concomitant damage suffered by monuments and ecclesiastical property, first during the Reformation and a century later in the disturbances accompanying the Civil Wars and the Protectorate, together with the relatively low esteem in which medieval art and architecture were widely held before the later eighteenth century, would argue in favour of a local reworking of old-fashioned, possibly damaged, monuments. That the stone was no longer available from a working quarry is suggested by the condition of the monuments. The eighteenth-century masons were apparently unfamiliar with Egglestone marble and consequently did not realize how ill-suited to incised inscriptions it was. The slabs, especially when newly quarried, were easily cut and formed an excellent carrying medium for brass effigies and plaques, as presumably the medieval masons well knew. The properties of the stone upon exposure to air seem to have escaped later patrons and masons: the originally readily-worked stone then develops a hardened 'skin' and becomes far more difficult to carve or cut. The shallowness of the inscribed lettering may attest to an ill-judged attempt to rework older monuments. Even if the stones were turned over for re-use, centuries of exposure to damp earth may have interacted with and damaged the surface structure.

Re-use of Egglestone marble slabs has been noted elsewhere. According to Blacker the dark coloured floor tiles in the nave of Ripon Cathedral were mainly Egglestone marble. It is also found in the cathedral at the entrances to the treasury and crypt and the modern, bevelled step from the crossing into the chancel. Blacker conjectures these may have come from recut grave slabs originally set in the floor of the church 'as has happened at York and Beverley Minsters'. Blacker also noted a grave slab dated 1811 that was cut from Egglestone marble and possibly re-used.[170]

The putative re-use of medieval memorials in the eighteenth century remains conjectural. What is evident is that there is a large, apparently anomalous, concentration of Egglestone marble in the parish church. Few of the stones remain in a medieval context; most carry eighteenth-century inscriptions, even though the quarries that produced the stone were active three to four centuries earlier. The surviving medieval memorials, being made of an expensive stone quarried elsewhere and worked in York, commemorate people of considerable status in the then small market town of Leeds. A number of medieval stone monument slabs identified by Thoresby in the early eighteenth century have since vanished, even though some of them had been augmented by ancillary memorial brasses let into them over the years, particularly in the seventeenth century. If a later, extensive re-use of the monumental slabs did indeed occur, why there should have been an apparent abrupt change of fashion among the most important families of the Leeds ruling oligarchy remains a mystery.

Walter Farquhar Hook, Sanctuary north side (detail). This effigy, showing all the naturalism typical of Victorian portrait sculpture, was carved
by W. D. Keyworth, Jr, of Hull. The monument, consisting of an effigy
recumbent on an elaborately carved neo-Gothic table tomb, was erected
in 1878, three years after Hook's death, at a cost of approximately £1000.
(*courtesy of* P. Gwilliam, ASWYAS)

William Beckett, Sanctuary south side (detail). Baron Carlo Marochetti,
one of the most fashionable sculptors of his day, carved this portrait of
William Beckett, a member of the prominent Beckett banking family,
and MP for Leeds for many years. (*courtesy of* P. Gwilliam, ASWYAS)

Watercolour by John N. Rhodes of Leeds, *c.* 1835: View in the old church of the north transept northward, showing the font and cover with the Royal Arms on the right. Note the monument to William Milner by Richard Fisher of York on the left (now in the north tower) and, opposite, the Royal Arms, commissioned by Ralph Thoresby early in the eighteenth century (now above the doorway leading from the north tower into the Lady Chapel). (*courtesy of* Leeds Library and Information Services)

Watercolour by John N. Rhodes of Leeds, *c.* 1835: Westward view in the old church of the chancel from the altar. Many of the monuments were moved into the new church. Note the hatchments on the ceilings of the side aisles. Of the many shown, only one survives in the new church: that painted with the arms of the Beckett family, now on the east wall of the north tower. (*courtesy of* Leeds Library and Information Services)

WOOD, FREDERICK JOHN

Sanctuary North Side, Wa.T. 5

A SINGLE ENGRAVED line borders this rectangular brass mural tablet. A five-petalled rosette is engraved after the dates 1881-1913; a four-petalled flower is engraved after the word 'CONVOCATION'; a stylized five-petalled flower is engraved after the words 'DR WOODFORD'. The tablet is 47.5 cm (h) by 76.5 cm (w).[27]

REMEMBER FOR GOOD, O GOD, THY SERVANT
FREDERICK JOHN WOOD M.A.
VICAR OF HEADINGLEY IN THIS CITY FOR 32 YEARS
1881 – 1913 ❁ HONORARY CANON OF RIPON MINSTER
AND PROCTOR IN CONVOCATION ✣ IN THIS PARISH
CHURCH HE HAD SERVED FOR 24 YEARS 1857 – 1881
UNDER DR HOOK, DR ATLAY, DR WOODFORD ❁ AND D^{R}
GOTT, TRUSTED BY THEM ALL, BELOVED BY THE PEOPLE
A "PRINCE OF CURATES"
THE PAVEMENT OF THIS SANCTUARY AND THE CANDELABRA WERE HIS GIFTS

HE FELL ASLEEP IN CHRIST 8. JULY *1913*

.."Other foundation can no man lay than is laid"..
.."In Thy light may he see light"..

HOOK, WALTER FARQUHAR

Sanctuary North Side, Table Monument

𝕭𝕺𝕽𝕹 † 𝕸𝕬𝕽𝕮𝕳 † 13 † 1798.

𝕸𝕬𝕷𝕿𝕰𝕽 † 𝕱𝕬𝕽𝕼𝕰𝕳𝕬𝕽 † 𝕳𝕺𝕺𝕶, † 𝕯.𝕯. † 𝕱.𝕽.𝕾.

𝕯𝕴𝕰𝕯 † 𝕺𝕮𝕿𝕺𝕭𝕰𝕽 † 20 † 1875,

𝕍𝕴𝕮𝕬𝕽 † 𝕺𝕱 † 𝕷𝕰𝕰𝕯𝕾, † 𝕬 † 𝕯. † 1837, ꞊ 1859.

THIS ELABORATE table monument is carved from white First Statuary Carrara and red, veined marble, the latter probably from Devon or Belgium. Dr Hook's effigy rests on an open tomb chest with cinquefoil arches. The base of the tomb chest contains a carved cross with the carved letters 'ihs' and foliate decoration. The effigy depicts a recumbent figure in clerical robes with hands held in prayer on his breast and his head resting on a pillow. His feet are laid on a cushion with two books. The monument was designed by Sir George Gilbert Scott and the effigy was carved by W. D. Keyworth, Jr. George Edmund Street designed the tomb chest, which was carved by Anthony Welsh of Leeds. The monument is signed: 'W. D. KEYWORTH, JUNR. 1878 LONDON & HULL'. *See photographs, pages 25 and 27.*

Walter Farquhar Hook was born in 1798, the son of a clergyman. His paternal grandfather had been an organist and composer in Norwich and his mother's father was a naval doctor and personal physician and advisor to George IV. Hook was schooled at Winchester and thence went on to Oxford. His first post was as curate at Moseley, Birmingham where he established a village school. In 1828 he applied for the living of Holy Trinity Church in Coventry, and it was there that he became acquainted with the new dissenting and urban working classes and where he resolved to set out on a mission to restore the parish church to a place at the heart of its community.

The Oxford Movement began in 1833. By then Hook already had firmly established views

as a high churchman, but found himself in sympathy with many of the precepts of the Tractarians although, as an instinctive conservative, he preferred to follow the old paths rather than demanding changes and reform. Hook was appointed vicar of Leeds in 1837. The Leeds Trustees who appointed him were themselves Tories who wanted a sound and effective man, in sympathy with their outlook, to be their next minister. On arrival in Leeds Hook found the old church unsuitable and in poor repair and instigated a programme that eventually resulted in the erection of a completely new and radically-designed building and one which was to prove immensely influential to church design throughout the country. Hook was seemingly indefatigable: the Parish Church of St Peter was only one of twenty-one churches he built in Leeds. His tenure in the town also saw the building of twenty-seven schools and twenty-three vicarages. At that time the parish church was situated in the midst of appalling slums and he worked hard throughout his ministry to alleviate the sufferings of his parishioners, particularly during the typhus and cholera epidemics of the 1840s. He also supported Lord Ashley's Ten Hours Bill against child labour.

In 1859 he left Leeds to become Dean of Chichester and it was there he died and was buried in 1875.[28] His tenure in Leeds had been so influential and well regarded that a monument to him was immediately proposed for the parish church. It was produced by Sir George Gilbert Scott, one of the most prominent designers of the time, at an estimated cost of £1000.[29]

STUDDERT KENNEDY, REVD GEOFFREY

South Aisle, Wa.T. 9 (Quiet Chapel)

THE CERAMIC FIGURE of 'Woodine Willie' is glazed white and depicts a clergyman wearing a plain cope with undecorated wide orphrey. It is mounted on a stand, which in turn is placed on a projecting rectangular shelf. The figure is 31 cm in height. The brass inscription plaque is mounted on the wall, below the figure and stand, and is 25 cm (h) by 28.1 cm (w).

The Revd Geoffrey Studdart Kennedy was born in Leeds, where his father was incumbent at St Mary's Quarry Hill. He was educated at Leeds Grammar School and Trinity College, Dublin. He trained as a clergyman and served as a curate, first in Rugby, then at Leeds Parish Church before taking the living of a poor parish in Worcester in 1914. He became an army chaplain in World War I, and it was then that he earned his nickname of 'Woodbine Willie' as he comforted wounded soldiers with cigarettes. He received the Military Cross at Messine Ridge after running into no-man's land to bring the wounded to safety whilst under heavy fire. He wrote a number of poems about his experiences during the war and these appeared in the books *Rough Rhymes of a Padre* (1918) and *More Rough Rhymes* (1919). His experiences during the war converted him to pacifism and Christian Socialism and he joined the Industrial Christian Fellowship to work to alleviate poverty, industrial unrest and unemployment in post-war Britain. He undertook speaking tours all over the country and it was during one of these that he was taken ill with influenza and died, aged forty-six.[47]

REMEMBER
THE LIFE AND MINISTRY
OF
THE REVEREND GEOFFREY STUDDERT KENNEDY M.C.
"WOODBINE WILLIE"
1883 – 1929
This Chapel of the Holy Spirit and St. Katharine
was furnished in his memory through the generosity
of friends and those inspired by his work and example
11th May 1986

10TH SERVICE BATTALION
PRINCE OF WALES'S OWN
WEST YORKSHIRE REGIMENT

South Aisle, Wa. T. 10 (Quiet Chapel)

IN REMEMBRANCE OF
THE OFFICERS·N.C.O^S & MEN
OF THE 10TH SERVICE BATT:
PRINCE OF WALES' OWN
WEST YORKSHIRE REG^T
WHO GAVE THEIR LIVES
WHILE SERVING
THEIR KING & COVNTRY
IN FLANDERS IN FRANCE
AND AT HOME
MCMXIV — MCMXIX
THIS TABLET IS SET VP BY
THEIR COMRADES

Nec aspera terrent

THE WHITE CRINOIDAL Hopton Wood limestone inscription tablet of this mural monument is set in a carved frame decorated with gilded acanthus leaves. It rests on a Hopton Wood limestone sill, below which is a curved apron made of green serpentinite. A circular yellow Belgian marble inset is applied to the centre of the apron. The inscription tablet is flanked by veined green pilasters, and is topped by a green stone frieze. A moulded pale grey Hopton Wood limestone cornice supports two gilded closed urns on either side, with a raised segmental pediment in the centre. The tympanum of the pediment contains an oval with the crest of the regiment (a raised, gilded running horse, surmounted by a gilded, carved Prince of Wales' plume) against a red background. The pediment is raised upon a pair of flat yellow marble pilasters.

In October 1924, the faculty of the Diocese of Ripon was petitioned to allow the erection of this monument, described at the time as 'a memorial tablet of alabaster and marble, approx. 5' x 2'10" [153cm (h) x 86.3 cm (w)] surmounted by the Crest of the Regiment'. [48]

BRASS EFFIGY OF A LADY

West End, WaT. 5

Tʜɪs ᴠᴇʀʏ ᴡᴏʀɴ brass shows the outline of a lady in a long full skirt and heart-shaped head-dress. Her hands are placed as if in prayer. The figure is 95 cm high. It is 27 cm wide at the base and 28.6 cm wide at the elbows. It is probably the brass originally set in the Nave, M.S. 19 (q.v.) and may commemorate a member of the Langton family.

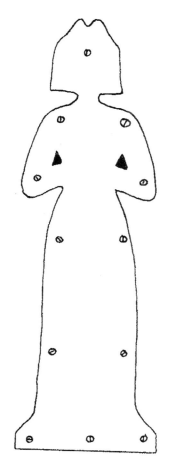

NEVINS, ARCHIBALD, SNR

West End, Wa.T. 6

Tʜɪs ʀᴇᴄᴛᴀɴɢᴜʟᴀʀ ʙʀᴀss mural tablet is 11.9 cm (h) by 18.5 cm (w). It is undecorated.

ALSO OF
Aʀᴄʜɪʙᴀʟᴅ Nᴇᴠɪɴs 𝔖ᴇɴɪᴏʀ,
who departed this Life,
the 21ˢᵗ. day of ApriL *1819,*
in the 32ⁿᵈ. Year
of his Age.

CHADWICK, JOSEPH

West End, Wa.T. 7

JOSEPH CHADWICK
OF THIS TOWN, DYER.
DEPARTED THIS LIFE OCT.R 9.TH 1845,
AGED 48 YEARS.

TO PERPETUATE THE REMEMBRANCE
OF THE MANY EXCELLENCIES
WHICH ADORNED HIS CHARACTER,
IN ALL THE VARIOUS RELATIONS OF LIFE
THIS TABLET
IS MOURNFULLY AND AFFECTIONATELY ERECTED.

THE WHITE First Statuary Carrara marble inscription tablet of this mural monument is mounted on a rectangular grey marble ground with an angled pedimental top. The incised letters of the inscription are filled with black. The inscription tablet is shield-shaped with a projecting, moulded cornice. A carved coat of arms (gules, an inescutcheon within an orle of martlets argent[53]) and wreath are set on the ground above the inscription tablet. The monument is signed 'WALSH & LEE, LEEDS'.

WOODWARD, JESSE

West End, Wa.T. 8

SACRED
TO THE MEMORY OF
JESSE WOODWARD, ESQUIRE,
OF THIS TOWN,
(LATE COLLECTOR OF EXCISE)
WHO DEPARTED THIS LIFE ON THE
11.TH DAY OF OCTOBER 1847,
AGED 76 YEARS.

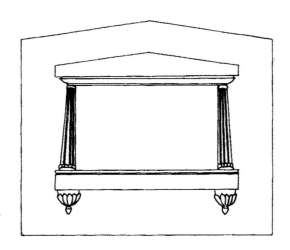

THIS MURAL MONUMENT has a white First Statuary Carrara marble sarcophagus-shaped inscription tablet set on a sympathetically shaped grey marble ground. A pair of fluted columns, supporting a projecting pediment, flanks the inscription tablet. The columns rest on a projecting sill, which is supported by a pair of carved pendants. The pendants terminate in pinecone drop finials. The monument is signed 'WILSON L[EE]D[S]'.

DIXON, JOHN

North Aisle, Wa.T. 7

THE WHITE INSCRIPTION tablet of this Second Statuary Carrara marble mural monument is set on an angular and curved grey veined Statuary Carrara marble ground. A white marble shield is applied to the apex of the ground's pyramidal top and is surmounted by a ribbon. A palm wreath is applied below the shield. A fluted, closed mourning urn, set on a gadrooned mount rests on the cornice of the inscription tablet. A double set of scrolled, carved pilasters flank the inscription tablet on each side. The pilasters terminate on claw feet, which rest upon a slightly projecting sill. A damaged and incomplete palm wreath is applied to the curved apron. The monument is signed 'Thos. Atkinson. York'.

The first member of the Dixon family in Leeds was Joshua, a younger son of John Dixon, of Heaton Royds, who was in the cloth trade. Joshua was born in the early seventeenth century and married Eleanor, the daughter of John Dodgson, alderman of Leeds. Eleanor's brother, also John Dodgson (q.v.) was mayor of Leeds in 1696 and 1710. Their eldest son, Jeremiah, married Mary Dodgson (the daughter of John Dodgson, the mayor) and it was their son John who died in 1749 and is commemorated here. John's son, Jeremiah Dixon, FRS, merchant and high sheriff of Yorkshire, commissioned this monument. In 1764 he purchased the estate of Gledhow from the Wilson family and in 1765 the manor of Chapel Allerton from the Killingbecks. Between 1766 and 1767 he commissioned John Carr of York to alter and extend the old house at Gledhow and surrounded it with elaborate plantations and gardens. John Carr had also probably designed Jeremiah Dixon's town house in Boar Lane between 1750–53 which has since been demolished.[62] His eldest son John (q.v.) was Colonel of the West Yorkshire Militia; his second son Jeremiah was mayor of Leeds in 1784 and married Mary, the daughter of John Smeaton, FRS, the civil engineer and builder of the Eddystone Lighthouse.[63]

According to the inscription John Dixon died 4 February 1749. The parish register, however, recorded his death 4 February 1748/9 and his burial 7 February 1748/9.

Thomas Atkinson of York, who made the monument, was primarily an architect, although he also made chimneypieces and

Near this Place
Are depoſited the Remains of
MR. JOHN DIXON of Leeds, *MERCHANT*,
Who died 4th Feby 1749, Aged 51 Years.
And alſo of FRANCES, his Wife,
Who died 16th Sep^r, 1750, Aged 62 Years.

Their exemplary conjugal Affection,
And uniform Practice of Religious Duties
Made their Loſs ſincerely lamented;
More Particularly by their only Son
JEREMIAH DIXON of Gledhow, Eſq^r, F.R.S,
High Sheriff of this County in the Year 1758,
Who died 7th June, 1782, Aged 56 Years.
At whoſe Requeſt this Monument is erected,
As a Token of Reſpect,
To the Memory of his Parents.

His own unſullied Purity and Amiableneſs of Manners,
Strict Integrity and Elegance of Taſte,
Cultivated Mind and Evenneſs of Temper,
With an unwearied Attention to the Duties
of a *MAN*, a *CITIZEN*, and a *CHRISTIAN*,
Engaged the Eſteem of all who knew him,
And rendered him an Example
Worthy the Imitation
of Poſterity.

monuments of 'good provincial workmanship' in Yorkshire and the North of England.[64] He designed the gothic front and gate-house of Bishopthorpe between 1763 and 1769 and died in 1798.

DIXON, MARY

North Aisle, Wa.T. 9

In Memory of
MARY DIXON, Wife of the above mentioned
JEREMIAH DIXON Eſq^r
and Daughter of the Revd HENRY WICKHAM,
RECTOR of *GUISELEY;*
who departed this life the 7th of April 1807,
Aged 73 Years.

"She was a bright example of Female excellence
in all the duties of a christian character
most perfect in
the most important."

THE RECTANGULAR inscription tablet of white Carrara marble of this mural monument is set in a plain rectangular Ashford black marble frame. The sill projects slightly to support the tablet. A pair of plain pilasters, topped with torus moulding, flanks the inscription tablet on either side.

DIXON, JOHN

North Aisle, Wa.T. 9

IN MEMORY
OF
JOHN DIXON, ESQ^RE.
OF GLEDHOW,
IN THIS COUNTY;
COLONEL OF THE 1ST WEST
YORK MILITIA;
WHO DIED IN LONDON APRIL 21ST 1824,
AGED 72 YEARS,
AND WAS BURIED
IN S^T MARY-LE-BONE CHURCH.

THE WHITE Carrara marble inscription tablet of this mural monument is set on a rectangular black ground with a hemispherical apron. The inscription tablet lies in a stylized sarcophagus-type frame with projecting cornice and sill. The sill rests on a pair of brackets. Each bracket is decorated with four carved tapering coniform pendants. A blank shield is applied to the ground and projects into the apron of the monument.

John Dixon was the eldest son of the wealthy merchant Jeremiah Dixon, FRS, of Gledhow Hall.

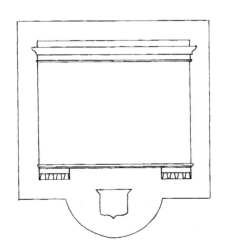

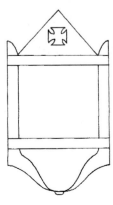

North Aisle Wa.T 11

SYKES, ELIZA

Altar Flats, M.S. 4

THIS MASSIVE SLAB of grey stone, which is possibly limestone, is 178.5 cm (l) by 96.5 cm (w).

SACRED
To the Memory of ELIZA,
Daughter of JOHN & HANNAH SYKES,
of Beech Grove,
who died 30th? of August 1842,
aged 7 Years and 5 Months.

"She is not dead but Sleepeth".

LEATHLEY, ELIZABETH

Altar Flats, M.S. 5

THIS MASSIVE slab of mid-grey stone (possibly limestone) is 185 cm (l) by 114 cm (w).

According to the *Parish Register of Burials,* 'John Leathley, Esqr of Woodhouse Barr,' died a sudden death aged seventy years.

HERE lieth inter'd the Body of
ELISABETH the Wife of
MR JOHN LEATHLEY in Hunſlet Lane
who died 23d Novr 1778.
in the 48th Year of her Age.
Alſo here lieth the Body of
MR JOHN LEATHLEY Huſband to the
above ELISABETH LEATHLEY.
who departed this Life the 11th of July
1803. in the 70th Year of his Age.

CARR, CHARLES

Altar Flats, M.S. 6

SACRED TO THE MEMORY OF
CHARLES CARR, M.D.
Sometime Physician to the
Infirmary in this Town.
Born at Bolton Abbey December the
17$\underline{th}$ 1769, he departed this Life at
Knowsthorpe House January 9$\underline{th}$ 1841.
Also of RACHEL his Wife, who died
11$\underline{th}$ of December 1845, aged *79* Years.

THIS MASSIVE slab of grey limestone is 178 cm (l) by 100.5 cm (w).

FENTON, ELIZABETH

Altar Flats, M.S. 7

HERE LIES INTERRED [ELIZABETH] FENTON
DAUGHTER OF M[R WILLIAM FENTON] OF
LEEDES WHO D[IED]   [AUGUST]
ANNO DOM 1714   YEAR
ALSO WILL
DYED Y^e 23   ANNO   1741
          AGED 22
ALSO ALICE
BELOVED WIFE
LIFE THE 19   [AUGUST]   1744   AGED
              63 YEARS
ALSO T
WAS TWICE
HE DIED

ALSO SARAH, YOUNGEST DAUGHTER TO
THE ABOVE M. W. FENTON WHO DIED
SEP^R 14TH 1759. AGED 38 YEARS
ALSO THOMAS HIS ELDEST SON WHO
DIED SEP^R THE 23^D *1774* AGED 66.
AND HANNAH HIS ELDEST DAUGHT^R
WHO DIED OCT^R 25TH *1777*. AGED 68.

THIS MASSIVE SLAB of Egglestone marble is 187.5 cm (l) by 102.5 cm (w). The inscription is very worn and is illegible in part. It can be partially reconstructed from the parish registers: 'Elizabeth, dau of Mr Wm Fenton of Medow lane', was buried on 4 August 1714; 'Alice, w. of Willm Fenton, Esq.,' was buried on 23 August 1744; Thomas Fenton, of Meadow Lane was buried on 28 September 1774.

William Fenton (1682–1749) (q.v.) was an alderman and mayor of Leeds in 1733 and 1747. He was a member of a large and important Leeds family and grandson of William Fenton of Woodhouse Hill, Hunslet, who was a merchant and was chief alderman in 1658.[75]

CALVERT, THOMAS

Altar Flats, M.S. 20

THIS MASSIVE slab of mottled dark grey crinoidal limestone is 179 cm (l) by 94 cm (w).

Thomas Calvert, of Headingley, was a dyer.[90]

𝔖 𝔄 ℭ ℜ 𝔈 𝔇
To the Memory of
Thomas Calvert,
of Headingley N͇ͬ Leeds who
Died February xvi[th] mdccliii,
Aged xlvii Years.

POLLARD, SAMUEL

Altar Flats, M.S. 21

THIS MASSIVE slab of mottled mid to dark grey shelly stone (possibly limestone), is 188.5 cm (l) by 100 cm (w).

Samuel (Soloman) Pollard, of Briggate, surgeon and alderman, was mayor of Leeds in 1714 and 1737. His wife, Judith, was one of the daughters of Henry Atkinson (q.v.), of Leeds.[91] According to the parish register she was buried on 27 March 1713. The *Parish Register of Burials* also recorded that of 'Mr Aldr Pollard, Brigt' on 27 February 1730/1.

Thomas Breary was the fourth son of the archdeacon of the West Riding and from a long-established York aldermanic family. He moved to Leeds 1715, was elected to the corporation in 1717 and became mayor in 1720. He moved from Leeds in 1730 and died without issue. Whilst in Leeds he was in partnership with Scudamore Lazenby, mayor in 1719,[92] and by 1725 is recorded as having a large house of three storeys and four bays (which could also have been used for business purposes) on Boar Lane at the corner of Cripplegate, adjacent to a bowling green. A group of crofts bearing his name was situated immediately behind the house.[93]

HERE lie
SOLOMAN POLLARD ESQ[R].
and JUDITH his Wife
She was interr'd April the 27th 171[3]
He was interr'd Feb[y] the 27th. 1731
Alſo ELISABETH their only Child
Relict of THOMAS BREAREY ESQ[R]
afterwards Widow of
HENRY ATKINSON ESQ[R]. of Caley
who departed this Life
Aug[t] 25th. 1782. aged 79.

SMITH, ANNE

Altar Flats, M.S. 22

IN MEMORY OF
ANNE CATHERINE JANE
WIFE OF JOHN SMITH ESQ^R BANKER, LEEDS,
WHO DIED 8TH OF JUNE 1854,
AGED 49 YEARS.

JOHN SMITH, BANKER, LEEDS

THIS MASSIVE mid to dark grey stone monument slab (probably limestone) is 181 cm (l) by 103 cm (w).

Anne Catherine Jane Smith was the first wife of John Smith, a partner in Beckett's Bank, Leeds. John Smith had originally come from Aberdeen to be the first manager of the Leeds Banking Company, which was founded in 1832. When William Beckett (q.v.) entered Parliament in 1841, the firm of Beckett and Co., deeply impressed by Smith, brought him into the partnership.[94] After Anne's death, John Smith married Mary Anne France (née Hopper) who was a great-niece of Samuel Kirshaw, DD (q.v.), vicar of Leeds, 1751–86.[95]

LAMBERTSON, SARAH

Altar Flats, M.S. 23

HERE LIETH THE BODY OF SARAH, THE
WIFE OF ROBERT LAMBERTSON, OF IBSEY
PITTS, WHO DIED MARCH THE 26TH 1757. ÆT. 70

ALSO SARAH, THE DAUGHTER OF THE
ABOVE ROBERT & SARAH LAMBERTSON
WHO DIED 30TH DECE^R 1785. AGED 64 YEARS.

ALSO SUSANNAH, THE DAUGHTER OF
EDWARD ARMITAGE OF HUNSLET LANE
WHO DIED 25TH MAY 1789. AGED 6 MONTHS

ALSO JAMES, THE SON OF EDWARD
ARMITAGE, WHO DIED 13TH OF JUNE 1792.
AGED 13 MONTHS.

ALSO JOSEPH, THE SON OF EDWARD
ARMITAGE, WHO DIED 27TH OF JUNE 1800,
AGED 10 MONTHS.

THIS MASSIVE monument slab of polished stone is 189 cm (l) by 112 cm (w). The slab is possibly Tournai Limestone.

Ibsey Pitts was probably in the area of Leeds also known as the Bank, as it is thus recorded as the residence of Sarah Lambertson in the *Parish Register of Burials*, March 1757.[96] The register also recorded the causes of the deaths of the three infants: Susannah and James both died of 'Fitts', while Joseph died of smallpox. By the time Joseph died, the family had moved from Hunslet Lane to South Parade.

IBBETSON, GEORGE

Nave, M.S. 3

THIS MASSIVE grey fossiliferous limestone ledger stone contains clear remains of crinoids, gastropods and corals. It is 199.5 cm (l) by 115.5 cm (w). Some of the inscription has been lost as the stone has been cut diagonally across the lower right corner to accommodate the lowest run of steps that lead to the sanctuary. The missing parts of the inscription have been taken from Rusby's transcription[100] and checked against the *Parish Register of Burials.*

The oval bas-relief achievement (65 cm in length by 55 cm wide) carved into centre top of the slab, shows the arms of the Ibbetsons: gules, on a bend cotised argent, three escallops of the field, impaling, ermine, on a pale sable three martlets in pale argent (Nicholson). The Ibbetson crest is a unicorn's head argent, powdered with escallops, horned, maned, and erased gules.[101]

According to the *Parish Register of Burials,* Mr George Ibbetson of Kirkgate was buried on 19 March 1732/3.

*H*ERE LIETH THE BODY OF MR GEORGE IBBETSON 4th SON OF IAMES IBBETSON Esq[R] OF LEEDES MERCHANT WHO DIED THE 15TH OF MARCH 1732. ÆTATIS *27.* ALSO THE BODY OF THE ABOVE S[D]. IAMES IBBETSON WHO DIED THE 16TH. OF OCTO[R] ANNO 1739   ÆTAT: 66 · ALSO INTERR'D IS THE BODY OF M[RS] ELIZABETH IBBETSON RELICT OF THE ABOVE JAMES IBBETSON WHO DEPART ED THIS LIFE ON THE 4TH. DAY OF NOVEM 1751 IN THE 81ST YEAR OF HER AGE. ALSO THEIR OLDEST DAUGHTER ELIZABETH THE WIFE OF SAMUEL DAVENPORT, WHO DIED APRIL 21ST. ANNO 1760.   ÆTATIS 61. AND ALSO THE REMAINS OF THE [SAID] SAMUEL DAVENPORT ESQ[R] AN A[LDERMAN] OF THIS BOROUGH WHO DIED S[EPTEMBER 13TH ANNO] *1777.* ÆTATIS 6[4]

IBBITSON, BARTHOLOMOW

Nave, M.S. 4

HERE *L*YETH [IN
TERRED THE BO]
DY OF [BARTHOLO]
MOW IBBITSON OF
LEEDS SHAMBLES
WHO DEPARTED
THIS LIFE THE 18TH
DAY OF OCTOBER
ANNO DOMINI
1676

THIS SHIELD-SHAPED brass monument slab is 25.2 cm (l) by 23 cm (w). Heating pipes obscure part of the inscription, which has been reconstructed from the transcription taken by Rusby.[102]

HEY, JOHN

Nave, M.S. 5

This rectangular brass tablet is 49 cm (l) by 42.5 cm (w) and has an engraved chevron border (1 cm wide, set 0.4 cm from the edge), which surrounds the inscription. Several lines of the inscription are covered by heating pipes and cannot be read.

William Hey (1736–1819) was an eminent surgeon and a man of extraordinary ability and determination. The second son of Richard Hey, drysalter of Pudsey, he lost the sight of his right eye at the age of four when the penknife he was using to try to cut a piece of string slipped. After attending the grammar school in Leeds he was apprenticed at fourteen to a Mr Dawson, surgeon and apothecary of Leeds, and completed his professional education in London in 1757 at St George's Hospital. He returned to Leeds as a surgeon and apothecary in 1759 and married Alice, the daughter of Robert Banks of Craven, with whom he had a large family. Appointed as one of the founding surgeons of the Leeds General Infirmary, he became its senior surgeon in November 1773. He was elected a Fellow of the Royal Society in 1775, was a close friend of Joseph Priestley and, in 1783, was the first president of the original Leeds Philosophical Society, which ceased to exist in 1788. He was lamed in 1778 when he was kicked by a horse but continued in his surgical practice. He was elected an alderman in 1786 and served as mayor of Leeds in 1787 and 1802. A philanthropist, he gave series of public lectures and courses and the resulting profits were presented to the Infirmary. He resigned his office as surgeon to the Infirmary on 7 October 1812 and was succeeded by his son the next day. His friend, the Revd Miles Atkinson (q.v.), preached the sermon at his funeral and he was buried at St Paul's, Leeds. A full length statue of him by

HERE lieth the Body of JOHN HEY, Son of WILLIAM HEY Eſqʳ who died May 20ᵀᴴ 1774. aged 8 Months. Alſo ROBERT BANKS HEY, Son of the aboveſaid WILLIAM HEY who died May 26ᵗʰ 177[4] Alſo SAMUEL HEY, another of his sons who died

And alſo ELIZABETH HEY, his Daughter, who died June 22ⁿᵈ 1783. aged One Year.
Alſo Mᴿ RICHARD HEY Surgeon. his eldeſt Son. who died March 20ᵗʰ 1789. aged 24 Years.
Alſo MISS ALICE HEY, Third Daughter of WILLIAM HEY, who Died Febʸ 24ᵗʰ 1794.
Aged 26 Years.

Chantrey was placed in the Infirmary and a portrait of him, by Allen, hangs in the boardroom there. His handsome brick house at the corner of Albion Street and Albion Place, Leeds, survives as the headquarters of the Leeds Law Society.[103]

According to the parish registers, John Hey, the son of Mr William Hey, Briggate, was born on 3 October 1773, was baptized 4 November and was buried 21 May 1774. Robert Banks Hey was born 29 August 1770, was baptized 27 September 1770 and was buried on 28 May 1774, just one week after his brother. 'Mr. Richard Hey, Single Man, of Briggate' died of consumption and was buried on 25 March 1789. The register recorded his age at death as twenty-six. 'Miss Alice Hey, Single Woman, of Briggate' died aged twenty-six, and was buried on 27 February 1794. She, like her brother Richard, died of consumption.

WAINHOUSE, MARGARET NEVINS

Nave, M.S. 17 (Choir)

THIS LARGE dark grey limestone slab is 185 cm (l) by 89.5 cm (w). The inscription 'We pray THEE help thy servants whom THOU has redeemed with thy precious blood –Make them to be numbered with thy saints in glory everlasting' is set around the outer edges of the monument. An embellished Latin cross fleurée has been carved onto the body of the slab and it is the base of the slab that carries the main part of the inscription.

We pray THEE help thy

glory everlasting in the saints with thy numbered be to Them

Servants whom THOU hast redeemed with thy

MARGARET NEVINS WAINHOUSE
DIED II MAY MDCCCXXIII
AGED XX YEARS
ROBERT WAINHOUSE
DIED III NOVEMBER MDCCCXX
AGED XXXIII YEARS.

Make - blood precious

BYWATER, THOMAS

Nave, M.S. 18

HERE LIETH THE BODY OF M THOMAS
BYWATER WHO DIED DEC THE 10 17[62]
AGED [68] YEARS
ALSO THE BODY OF PHEBE HIS WIFE
WHO DIED AUG. 27 1768. AGED 77 YEARS.
ALSO THE BODY OF M. RICH. BYWATER
SON OF THE ABOVESAID THO. AND PHEBE
BYWATER, WHO DIEDTHE 15TH FEBY 1788
AGED 64 YEARS.
Alſo SARAH Wife of the above
RICHARD BYWATER
who died March 1[3] 1807 aged 8[5] Years.
Alſo SARAH KILLERBY
who departed this Life November
the 18th 1824 aged 76 Years.

THIS LARGE Egglestone marble slab is very worn and some of the inscription has been lost. It is 184 cm (l) by 104.5 cm (w).

The inscription has been reconstructed according to Rusby's transcription[117], and checked against the parish registers. Thomas Bywater of Back Shambles was buried on 12 December 1762. Sarah Bywater 'widow of Kirkgate' died aged eighty-five of old age and was buried on 18 March 1807.

LANGTON? INDENT OF A LADY

Nave, M.S. 19 (Choir)

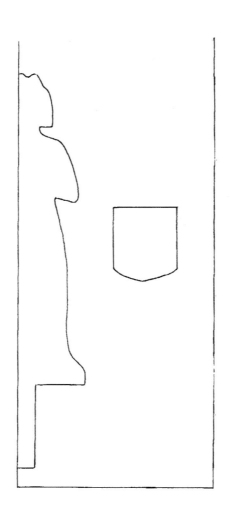

ONLY HALF of this Egglestone marble slab is visible: much of the slab is hidden under the choir stalls. The exposed stone measures 185 cm (l) by 53 cm (w). It bears no inscription; only the indents remain showing the outline of a lady in a dress and with a heart-shaped head-dress. A rectangular indented area is carved below the hem of her dress; the indent of a shield 16.5 cm (l) by 14.5 cm (w) is set beside her elbow. Other, very worn shield-shaped indents are faintly discernable along the right margin of the slab.

This may be the monument described by Thoresby as containing 'the effigies of John Langton, Esq; [sic] and his Wife, inlaid in Brass, with Vacancies for 12 Escutcheons, which have been barbarously torn off; as is also the Head of his Statue'[118] although such escutcheon-shaped indents as remain on the slab are now worn and barely visible. Thoresby, however, only recorded two stone slabs that still contained medieval brass figurative effigies in his time: those for Sir John and Lady Langton (now M.S. 20 and South Aisle, Wa.T. 1) and for John Langton, Esq., and his wife Agnes (inscription plate now placed in the South Aisle, Wa.T. 2). None of the other medieval brass effigies had apparently survived by the time he came to record the monuments of the parish church. The brass effigy of the lady has been affixed to the west wall of the Church (West End, Wa.T. 5).

IBBETSON, CATHARINE

Nave, M.S. 32 (North Crossing)

THE INSCRIPTION of this monument is incised on a massive slab of Egglestone marble, 176 cm (l) by 101.3 cm (w). The indent of a shield is set in the monument at top centre and shows signs of having once contained a brass plaque: six round holes have been drilled around the periphery of the indent which is 25 cm (l) by 23.6 cm (w). It is undecorated. The inscription is worn and has been reconstructed with the aid of the parish registers and contemporary newspaper accounts.

Catharine was the first wife of Sir Henry Ibbetson, a very wealthy man whose father had made a fortune in the woollen trade between 1695 and 1739. Although he was a second son, he succeeded to his father's property, which after 1739 provided him with an income of over £1000 p.a. from land alone.[122] Catharine Ibbetson's obituary notice in the *Leeds Mercury* Tuesday October 21 1740 reflects the family's prominence: 'On Friday Night last dy'd much lamented at Red Hall near This Town, the Lady of Henry Ibbetson, Esq: Daughter of Francis Fulgham, Esq: near Rotherham, a Gentlewoman of an extra ordinary Character, and greatly esteem'd by all her Acquaintance. Her Corpse was interr'd yesterday afternoon, at the Parish Church of St. Peter's, in this Town.'

Henry became increasingly involved in politics from the 1740s and, at the time of the 1745 Rebellion he raised, at his own expense, one hundred men for the defence of his county and in return was awarded a baronetcy in 1748. In 1741 he made an advantageous marriage to Isabella, the eldest daughter of Ralph Carr of Durham who was, according to the report in the *Leeds Mercury* 'a beautiful young lady of good Fortune …' and the couple had ten children. He was high sheriff in 1748, was elected mayor 1752–3 and gradually withdrew from the family cloth-making business, knowing his son would inherit his elder brother's estate at Denton, near Ilkley.[123]

Mrs Thomasin Paxton was Lady Isabella's aunt. The notice of her death in the *Leeds Intelligencer* on 8 March 1757 described her as 'a maiden gentlewoman, aunt to the Lady of Sir Hy. Ibbetson, Bart.' she died at her house in 'Hunslit Lane'.

HERE LIETH ALSO THE BODY OF CATHARINE IBBETSON WIFE OF HENRY IBBETSON Esqr DAUGHTER OF FRANCIS FOLJAMBE OF ALDWARKE ESq^r WHO DEPARTED THIS LIFE 17— OCTOB^R 1740   ÆT [23]

ELIZABETH DAUGHTER OF Sr HENRY IBBETSON BAR^T DEPARTED THIS LIFE THE 9THOF JUNE 17[52]   Æ [4]

ALSO CATHARINE HIS DAUGHTER WHO DEPARTED THIS LIFE THE [12TH] OF MAY 17[5]4 AGED 5 MONTHS M^{RS} THOMASIN PAXTON LATE OF THE CITY OF DURHAM OB.7 MARCH 1757   ÆT 69: DAME ISABELLA IBBETSON WIFE TO S^R HENRY IBBETSON OF THIS TOWN BAR^T OB 21 JUNE 1757   ÆT 34 HERE LIETH THE REMAINS OF Sr HENRY IBBETSON BARONET WHO DIED THE 22ND DAY OF JUNE *1761* AGED 55 YEARS

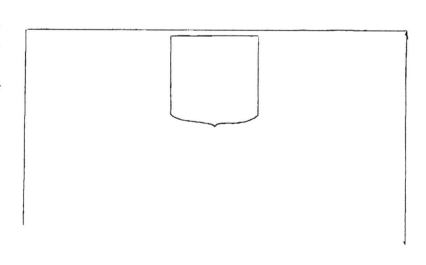

IBBITSON, JAMES

Nave, M.S. 33 (North Crossing)

HERE LIETH INTERRED THE BODY
OF MR JAMES IBBITSON LATE CLOTH
WORKER IN LEEDS VICKERLANE WHO
DEPARTED THIS LIFE Y^E 25TH OF AUGUST
ANNO 1661
ALSO HERE LYETH INTERRED Y^E BODY
OF M^{RS} MARY IBBITSON WIFE TO THE
ABOVESAID MR JAMES WHO DEPARTED
THIS LIFE THE 24 DAY OF [OCTOBER 1685]
A[GED 80 YEARS]
ALSO HERE IS INTERRED THE BODY OF
MR JOSHUA IBBETSON SON TO MR JAMES
LATE ALDERMAN AND [MAYOR OF THIS
CORPORATION] ANNO 16[85] WHO DEPARTED
THIS LIFE THE 11TH OF FEBRUARY ANNO D [1700]
AGED 57 YEARS
ALSO [FIVE CHILDREN OF THE ABOVESAID
MR JOSHUA IBBETSON IS HERE INTERRED
3 SONNS AND 2 DAUGHTERS]

Also M^{RS} Mary Ibbetson WIFE TO
THE ABOVESAID ALD^M Ibbetson AND
DAUGHTER TO CLL^R Brearey Esq
Lord Major of the Citty OF Yorke
anno *1669* WHO DEPARTED THIS LIFE Y^E
22nd March 1715 Aged 74.

THIS GREY limestone monument slab is 176.5 cm (l) by 99 cm (w). The incised lettering is badly worn and the words are indecipherable in some areas. Where possible, the inscription has been reconstructed using the transcriptions taken by Thoresby and Rusby,[124] with the dates checked in the parish registers.

According to the *Parish Register of Burials* 'Ald^r Jos^a Ibbetson of Kirkg^t' was buried on 13 February 1700/1 and 'Mrs Mary Ibbetson, Simpson fould, wid:' was buried on 24 March 1715/6.

GARDINER, SAMUEL

Nave, M.S. 34 (North Crossing)

Here lyes the Body of m^r
Samuel Gardiner of this Town
Mercht who dyed Augt ye 17th 1717
Aged 27

THIS GREY limestone floor slab is 176.5 cm (l) by 97.5 cm (w).

The *Parish Register of Burials* intriguingly recorded that 'Mr. Sam^{ll} Gardner, Batchler, dy'd att Mrs Hey, in hunslet lane'. He was buried on 19 August 1717.

HALL, JOHN

Nave, M.S. 35 (North Crossing)

THIS GREY limestone slab is 176.5 cm (l) by 98 cm (w). The inscription is very worn and is illegible in part.

John Hall, a wine merchant, was born in 1741. His brother, Henry, (q.v.) was mayor of Leeds in 1796. John Hall was married to Ann Tidswell (born 1757) the daughter of Samuel Tidswell (q.v.), wine merchant of Leeds. [125]

SACRED
TO THE MEMORY OF JOHN HALL, OF
THIS TOWN GENTLEMAN WHO DEPARTED
THIS LIFE MARCH 13TH 1813. AGED 72.
ALSO OF ANN HALL, WIFE OF THE ABOVE
WHO DEPARTED THIS LIFE NOV[R] 21ST 1822.
AGED 65 YEARS.
ALSO OF ANN THEIR DAUGHTER
WHO DEPARTED THIS LIFE JUNE 1-, 179-.
AGED 10 YEARS

TIDSWELL, RICHARD

Nave, M.S. 36 (North Crossing)

THIS GREY limestone floor slab is 176.5 cm (l) by 100.5 cm (w). The lower part of the inscription has been cut and the words have been restored according to Rusby's transcription. [126]

Richard and Margaret Tidswell lived at Simpson's Fold. Their son, Samuel, was a wine merchant in Leeds and it was his daughter Ann who married John Hall (q.v.), another wine merchant and member of a long-established and prominent Leeds family. [127]

IN MEMORY OF
RICHARD TIDSWELL who died 2nd Dec[r]
1750 aged 70 Years
MARGARET TIDSWELL who died 20th July
1753 aged 69 Years
SAMUEL TIDSWELL who died 1-[th] April
1771 aged 45 Years
ELIZABETH Wife of the above Samuel
Tidswell who died 17 December 1782
aged 55 Years.
ELIZABETH 2nd Daughter of the above
Samuel and Elizabeth and Widow of
WILLIAM BROOKS Esq[r] of Oporto who
died 27th October 1837 aged 78 Years
ELIZABETH MARGARETTA BROOKS
their Grand Daughter who died 12th March
1824 aged 13 Years
ANN WATSON Daughter of the late
TIMOTHY WATSON of this Town and
Niece to Elizabeth Tidswell who died
29th March 1821 aged 79 Years.

[Other] Members of the family are interred in the Church [of St Mary's, Aldersgate Parish,] in the city of L[ondon]

KENION, PHOEBE

Nave, M.S. 48

THE INSCRIPTION is engraved onto a nowy-headed brass slab, 35 cm (l) by 27.5 cm (w). The engraved lettering and decoration are coloured black. The letters are embellished with scrolls and a black border surrounds the inscription.

Phoebe was the wife of alderman Edward Kenion, apothecary, who was mayor in 1731 and 1746.[135] Their son, Edward Kenion, merited the following obituary in the *Leeds Intelligencer*: 'Last week died Edward Kenion, junior, Merchant in this Town, an affectionate Husband, a tender Parent, a faithful Friend, and a cheerful Companion.'[136] Another son, James, (q.v.), was a surgeon and was mayor of Leeds in 1766.

Here Lieth
Inter'd in Hopes of a Joyfull
Resurrection the Body of Phœbe Wife
to Mr Edward Kenion Jun. who depart
ed this Life the 19th Day of August 1747
Aged 22 years
Also the Body of M. Edward Kenion
Jun. who Departed this Life the 30, of March
1756 in the 35th, year of his Age.
Also the Body of Ann Kenion Youngest
Daughter of the above Edward Kenion
who Departed this Life the 8th. of Dec.
1760 Aged 5 Years

Also the Body of Mary, Widow
of the above Edward Kenion Jun:
who departed this Life the 21st Day
of March 1796 Aged *75* Years.

DAVISON, MARY

Nave, M.S. 49

THIS RECTANGULAR bronze tablet is placed together with M.S. 50 and M.S. 51, so it forms the bottom-most of three separate panels. The lettering is cast and raised. This single tablet is 20 cm (l) by 24.5 cm (w).

ALSO
THE REMAINS OF
MARY
RELICT OF
THE ABOVE NAMED
ROBERT DAVISON
WHO DIED APRIL 6TH 1832
AGED 86 YEARS

MACKENZIE, KENNETH TAIT

Nave, M.S. 50

Kenneth Tait Mackenzie
Died March 17ᵗʰ 1815
Aged 14 Years
Grandson of the above
Robert Davison

THIS RECTANGULAR bronze tablet, 18.1 cm (l) by 24.5 cm (w), is placed between M.S. 49 and M.S. 51 to form what appears to be a single floor slab monument with overall dimensions of 59.1 cm (l) by 24.5 cm (w). The lettering is cast and raised.

DAVISON, ROBERT

Nave, M.S. 51

THE REMAINS OF
Robert Davison.M.D.
Who Departed this Life
the 12ᵗʰ Augᵗ 1810
Aged 66
Allso the Remains of2of his Sons

THIS BRONZE PANEL, 20.2 cm (l) by 24.5 cm (w), forms the uppermost of a set of three abutted memorials (together with M.S. 49 and M.S. 50) so they appear to form one continuous floor slab. The monument is cast and the letters of the inscription are raised.

Robert Davison was a physician at the Infirmary and lived in East Parade at the time of his death.[137] In November 1800 he was one of the medical men who offered to vaccinate the poor of Leeds free of charge in order to contain a virulent outbreak of smallpox which was then sweeping through the town.[138]

WILKINSON, ZECHARIAH

Nave, M.S. 52

THE INSCRIPTION on this stone slab is obscured in part by the pew placed over it. The slab is approximately 210 cm (l) and 142.8 cm (w).

Zechariah Wilkinson was a prominent clothier in Leeds.[139] His wife, described in the *Parish Register of Burials* as 'Mrs. Sarah Wilkinson, widow of Albion Street', died aged seventy-seven years 'of a decline'. She was buried on 14 March 1810.

𝕾𝕬𝕮𝕽𝕰𝕯 𝕿𝕺 𝕿𝕳𝕰 𝕸𝕰𝕸𝕺𝕽𝖄

of ZECHARIAH WILKINSON, of Osmondthorp, who departed this Life the 18th Day of Jany. 1797, aged 60 Years.
Also SARAH, Wife of the above ZECHARIAH
[............MARCH 1810]

1810, aged 77 Years.
Also MARY ANN WILKINSON, Wife of WILLIAM WILKINSON, Merchant of this Town who departed this Life April 10th 1831, aged 49 Years.
Also WILLIAM WILKINSON, Son of the above ZECHARIAH and SARAH WILKINSON, who departed this Life Jany, 18th1832, aged 58 Years.

SMITH, JOHN

Nave, M.S. 53

THIS STONE monument slab is 186.4 cm (l) by 112.7 cm (w).

According to the *Parish Register of Burials* Mr John Smith, married man of Kirkgate, was buried 1 April 1799, aged seventy-one. He was said to have died of the flux. His wife Ann, also living in Kirkgate at the time of her death eleven years later, died of 'a decline'.

Here lieth interred the Body of IOHN SMITH Esq of this Town Merchant who died the —-day of March *1799*, aged *71* Years.
Alſo ANN Wife of the ſaid IOHN SMITH Esq who died the 11th day of March 1810, aged 83. Years.

Although Thomas Lloyd died at the estate he had acquired near Pickering, a public meeting was held in Leeds at the time of his death and it was resolved 'That as a due mark of respect for the invaluable services of the late Colonel Lloyd to this town and neighbourhood, a monument should be erected to his memory by subscription in the parish church.' The resolution was seconded by Christopher Beckett (q.v.) and carried unanimously; a committee was formed and about £200 was subscribed directly at the meeting.[156]

The sculptor chosen for the monument was Joseph Gott (1786-1860), a second cousin of Benjamin Gott (q.v.) and a pupil of John Flaxman. When the monument was eventually erected in the parish church in 1834 (in the south side 'immediately under the painted window') it was greatly admired. According to the *Leeds Mercury* on 22 March 1834 'It is constructed of beautiful white marble; and the inscription … is surmounted by an admirable bust of the deceased.'

BRAMELD, ETHEL JANE

Lady Chapel, Wa.T. 3 (South Wall)

•𝕿𝔬•𝔱𝔥𝔢•𝔊𝔩𝔬𝔯𝔶•𝔬𝔣•𝔊𝔬𝔡•
AND·IN·MEMORY·OF
ETHEL·JANE·BRAMELD
WHO·FOR·28·YEARS·WAS·A·FAITHFUL
WORKER·FOR·GOD·IN·THIS·PARISH·AND
DURING·THE·CLOSING·YEARS·OF·HER
LIFE·FOR·THE·ADVANCEMENT·AL^SO·OF
HIS·KINGDOM·IN·THE·ISL^ES·OF·THE·SEA

♠   ♠   ♠

She was born on All Saints Day 1858
and entered into Reſt July 19 : 1907:
R · I · P

THIS DOMED-HEADED brass tablet has a reversed arch base and is 59 cm (h) by 38.2 cm (w). A Latin cross is engraved above the inscription. An extra arm extends downwards to the right. Each arm terminates in a six-pointed star and each star contains a large cut and facetted brilliant crystal. The Greek letters Φ Z Σ H are engraved in each of the four major arms of the cross; Ω is engraved at the centre of the cross. Three engraved spades separate the main body of the inscription from the text beginning with 'She was born … '.

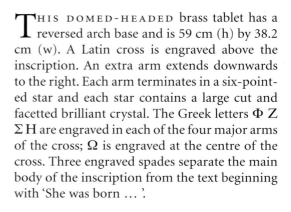

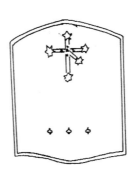

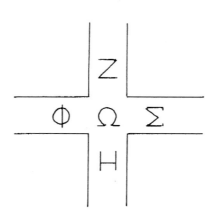

OATES, LAWRENCE EDWARD GRACE

Lady Chapel, Wa. T. 15 (South Wall)

THIS RECTANGULAR brass mural tablet is 62.7cm (h) by 46.3 cm (w). The letters of the engraved inscription are coloured black. The translation of the Greek inscription is: the grave of illustrious men is the entire world.

In March 1913, once the news of the disastrous end of the Scott expedition was known to the public, the local press proposed that a memorial for Captain Oates should be erected in Leeds Parish Church and this was endorsed in the churchwardens' meetings by Edwin Kitson Clark (q.v.). The Oates family had had long associations with Leeds, though Lawrence Edward Grace Oates was from the Kent branch of the family. This memorial plaque was dedicated after evensong 30 October 1913.[166]

IN MEMORY OF
LAWRENCE EDWARD GRACE OATES
CAPTAIN 6TH (INNISKILLING) DRAGOONS
BORN 17TH MARCH 1880
WHO HAVING SERVED HIS COUNTRY WITH DISTINCTION
IN THE SOUTH AFRICAN WAR 1901-2
JOINED CAPTAIN SCOTT'S ANTARCTIC EXPEDITION 1910
REACHING THE SOUTH POLE 17TH JANUARY 1912
AND ON THE RETURN JOURNEY LAT. 80: 8', 8".
IN THE HOPE OF SAVING THE LIVES OF HIS COMPANIONS
GAVE HIS OWN LIFE
17TH MARCH 1912
THIS MONUMENT IS PLACED HERE BY FELLOW CITIZENS
AS A RECORD OF THE BRAVE ACT OF
"A VERY GALLANT GENTLEMAN"
A.D. 1913.

ἀνδρῶν ἐπιφανῶν πᾶσα γῆ τάφος

BODINGTON, SIR NATHAN

Lady Chapel, Wa.T. 16 (South Wall)

IN•MEMORY•OF
SIR•NATHAN•BODINGTON•LITT.•D.
BORN•AD•1848•AT•WITTON•IN•WARWICKSHIRE.
SOMETIME•FELLOW•OF•LINCOLN•COLL•OXFORD.
BEING•CHOSEN•AS•PRINCIPAL•of•the•YORKSHIRE•COLLEGE•HE•WITH•HIS•COLLEAGUES
ON • COUNCIL • AND • SENATE • DILIGENTLY • WATCHED • OVER • ITS • GROWTH • FOR
TWENTY-ONE YEARS • ON • THE • FOUNDATION • of • the • UNIVERSITY • of • LEEDS • BY
ROYAL·CHARTER • in • the • REIGN • of • KING • EDWARD • VIITH • HE·BECAME • in•AD• *1904*
FIRST•VICE•CHANCELLOR.
AFTER•SERVING•in•that•OFFICE•SEVEN•MORE•YEARS•HE•DIED•at•LEEDS•12TH•MAY • 1911.
A • MASTER • OF • EDUCATION • HE •BROUGHT • TO • ITS • DEVELOPMENT •IN •THIS •CITY •TENACITY •OF
PURPOSE • UNCEASING • CARE • WIDE • KNOWLEDGE • AND • THE • EXAMPLE • of
a • GOOD • LIFE• WHEREBY •HE•WAS•ENABLED•UNDER •THE •GOOD •PROVIDENCE
OF • GOD • TO • SEE • HIS • WORK • ESTABLISHED • ON •A • FIRM • FOUNDATION.
HE • MARRIED • ELIZA • THIRD • DAUGHTER • O F • SIR • JOHN • BARRAN • BART.

This large brass rectangular mural tablet is 45.5 cm (h) by 87 cm (w). The engraved lettering and decoration are filled with black. In each of the four corners there is an engraved spade-shaped shield. All the shields are identical in size and decorated with heraldic devices. The shield in the upper left corner bears the arms of the University of Leeds; its motto is contained within the open pages of a book:

ET SCI
AVGE EN
BITVR TIA.

The shield in the upper right corner contains an open book with the motto:

DOMI MINA
NVS TIO
ILLV MEA.

Family coats of arms fill the lower two corners.

JOWETT, ABIGAIL

Lady Chapel, Wa.T. 23 (West Wall)

THIS RECTANGULAR Carrara marble mural tablet is 31.3 cm (h) by 48.3 cm (w). The incised letters of the inscription are coloured black.

Here lieth Interr'd the Body of
Abigail, Wife of Mr I^o Jowett,
~~Daughter of Martin~~
Huntington of Holbeck Gen^t
She departed this life y^{e}13$^{th.}$
Day of Septem^r *1764.*
Aged 63 Years.

LADY CHAPEL DEDICATION

Lady Chapel, Wa.T. 24 (Staircase)

THIS BRASS TABLET, which is 24.8 cm (h) by 27.4 cm (w), has white script on a black enamelled background. Decorative scrollwork is centred under the inscription.

The Lady Chapel was rededicated as a memorial chapel after World War I. The massive stone monument to Christopher Beckett was dismantled to make room for the carved and gilded oak reredos. At the same time black and white marble tiles were laid on the floor at the east end of the chapel. The architect in charge of the works was F. C. Eden.[181]

THE ALTAR, REREDOS, CREDENCE
TABLE AND OTHER ORNAMENTS
OF THIS CHAPEL WERE DEDICATED
ON TUESDAY, MARCH 28TH 1922,
TO THE GLORY OF GOD AND IN
MEMORY OF THE MEN OF LEEDS
PARISH CHURCH WHO FELL IN THE
WAR & IN THANKSGIVING FOR THOSE
WHOSE LIVES WERE PRESERVED

BARSTOW, ELIZABETH

Lady Chapel, Wa. T. 25 (North Wall)

[Momento Mori
Death neither youth nor age doth spare,
Therefore to follow me prepare;
Whilst life doth last, lett peitie
(As it was mine) yoᵣ practice be
Let virtue crown yoᵣ days, and then
We happily shall meet again]

Adjacent is ye Body of Elizabeth [ye vertious]
Wife of M. JEREMIAH BARSTOW of Leeds
Who departed this life [ye 4ᵗʰ day of Feb
1698 in ye twenty-eighth year of her age]
Also [three of their sonns]
Also Yᵉ Sᵈ [Jer] Barstow Esq [twice]
Mayor of this borough [obiit 2]
.......Die May 1734 Æt 72

DESCRIBED BY Thoresby as 'a handsome Monument of the white Free Stone'[182] this stone mural monument is in the form of a carved baroque cartouche set on a black ground. A cherub's head is set at the top centre above the inscription tablet, which is flanked by drapery. A pendant hanging from the main body of the monument contains another cherub's head, again carved in high relief. The monument is in poor repair and the inscription is virtually illegible. It was reconstructed from the transcriptions made by Thoresby and Rusby[183] and checked against the parish registers.

The *Register of Burials* recorded the burial of Elizabeth the wife of 'Mr Jere: Barstow, of Kirkgatend', on 6 February 1698/9. Jeremiah Barstow, alderman and mayor of Leeds in 1706 and 1724, was buried on 5 May 1734.

KILVINGTON, DOROTHY

Lady Chapel, Wa. T. 26 (North Wall)

SACRED
TO THE MEMORY OF
DOROTHY KILVINGTON
WIFE OF JERᴴ BARSTOW ESQ
WHO DIED MARCH 15ᵀᴴ 1803.

THIS MURAL TABLET with domed top and carved corners has a straight lower edge with an armourial shield set below.[184] A winged cherub's head supports the tablet and shield. The inscription tablet is surrounded by carved acanthus leaf borders with more scrolled acanthus leaves surrounding the whole. These descend from scrolling on the upper part of the frame.

BARSTOW, ALICE

Lady Chapel, Wa.T. 27 (North Wall)

THIS MURAL MONUMENT is 132 cm (h) by 74.5 cm (w). It is carved from what might be Carrara marble, though cleaning would be required before identification can be made with certainty. The monument consists of a round tablet in a round frame, carved with flowers and supported below by leaves and a foliate head ('Green Man'), whose face peers out from the centre. Below the head is a bracket with acanthus leaf carved decoration, and at the top of the frame are two cherubs' faces with wings, carved either side of an heraldic shield which contains the Barstow arms.

SACRED
TO THE MEMORY OF
M^{RS.} ALICE BARSTOW, WIDOW,
AND DAUGHTER OF
JOHN DOUGLAS ESQUIRE,
OF AUSTROP HALL.
WHO DEPARTED THIS LIFE
NOVEMBER 15TH. 1712. ÆTATIS 77.

BURMA CAMPAIGN

Lady Chapel, Wa.T. 28 (North Wall)

THIS BRASS INSCRIPTION tablet is mounted upon a wooden plaque 33.5 cm (h) by 42.5 cm (w). The engraved letters of the inscription are filled with black. A cast brass Burma Star badge is affixed between the dates and the badge is decorated with coloured enamels.

IN MEMORY

of those who died and
all who served in the

BURMA CAMPAIGN
1941 1945

When you go home – tell them of us and say
"For your tomorrow – we gave our today"

BURMA STAR ASSOCIATION
LEEDS BRANCH

DUNWELL, SUSANNA

Lady Chapel, Wa. T. 39 (Window Sills)

THIS SHIELD-SHAPED brass tablet is 40 cm (h) by 36 cm (w). The raised inscription is contained within an embossed oval in the centre of the shield. Naïve angels with outstretched wings are delineated in the two upper corners. Swags of husks descend from simple scrolling on either side of the central oval.

MEMORIÆ SACRÆ
SUSANNÆ UXORIS
MICHAELIS DUNWELL
QUÆ OBIJT 11 APRILIS
DOM: 1699
ANNO {
ÆTAT: 19

THORESBY, JOHN

Lady Chapel, Wa. T. 40 (Window Sills)

THIS BRASS TABLET is shield-shaped and is 21 cm (h) by 17.5 cm (w). The engraved inscription is very worn and only the one line with the date could be deciphered with certainty. The rest of the inscription has been taken from Rusby's transcription.[196]

John Thoresby, merchant and chief alderman of Leeds was born in December 1593. The son of a prosperous yeoman, he came to Leeds from the East Riding and made a good marriage to Grace Cloudsley who died in 1646.[197] Their son was John Thoresby (q.v.), the father of Ralph (q.v.) the antiquary.

[To the memory of Mr. John Thoresby, who died Sep 20, 1661, Ætat 69.

Here lies lamented, precious dust,
A tradesman true, a justice just,
A husband kind, a parent dear,
Who walked with God, in faith and fear,
As also Grace, his gracious wife,
Who for a better chang'd her life]

MAY 24 1616

[They lived in love, and dy'd in hope to have
A joyful resurrection from the grave.]

SKELLTON, THOMAS

Lady Chapel, Wa.T. 41 (Window Sills)

HERE LYETH BVRIED THE BODIES OF THREE
CHILDREN OF HENRY SKELLTON OF OSMONDTHORP
GENTLEMAN THOMAS AND HENRY WAS BVRIED
THE 24TH DAY OF OCTOBER AND WILLIAM
THE 26TH DAY OF OCTOBER ANNO DOMINI 1660
∽∽SIC TRANSIT GLORIA MVNDI <<<<

THIS PLAIN BRASS tablet is 15.6 cm (h) by 27.5 cm (w). It has curved lower edges and the last line of script is decorated with engraved scrolls and chevrons. It was originally set on a stone in the north choir of the old church.[198]

Henry Skellton was mayor of Leeds in 1664 and 1680. Thomas, Henry and William Skellton were three of the children he had with his wife Ellen (died in November 1693), the daughter and co-heiress of William Marshall (q.v.) of Moor Allerton. At least five other children survived their parents. Henry died on 20 November 1701, aged eighty-three years. The family had had extensive lands in Osmondthorpe for many generations: a William Skelton was recorded as living there in 1383. In the eighteenth century the family sold their land holdings to James Ibbotson (q.v.), of Leeds.[199]

MIDGLEY, MARY

Lady Chapel, Wa.T. 42 (Window Sills)

ALSO
MARY YE 2D WIFE OF YE SD ROBT MIDGLEY.
DAUGHTER OF SR JOHN COX KNIGHT.
WHO
UPON YE 20TH OF APL 1758 IN HER 90TH YEAR
DIED
THE DEATH OF THE RIGHTEOUS AND
MAY OUR LATTER END BE LIKE HERS

THIS PLAIN, rectangular brass tablet with engraved lettering is 18 cm (h) by 24 cm (w).

LEIGH, ROGER HOLT

Lady Chapel, Wa.T. 53 (North Wall)

SACRED TO THE MEMORY OF
ROGER HOLT LEIGH, ESQUIRE
TWENTY SEVEN YEARS A MEMBER OF THE CORPORATION,
AND A STRENUOUS SUPPORTER OF THE INSTITUTIONS OF THE BOROUGH OF LEEDS.
HE WAS A WARM ADVOCATE OF THE ESTABLISHED CHURCH, AN UNCOMPROMISING DEFENDER
OF THE GLORIOUS CONSTITUTION OF 1688, A CONSISTENT PATRIOT, AND A FAITHFUL FRIEND.
DURING THE GENERAL ELECTION IN THE YEAR 1831,
WHILST ENGAGED IN THE EXERCISE OF HIS FRANCHISE AS A BURGESS OF WIGAN, HIS NATIVE PLACE,
HE WAS SO SEVERELY INJURED BY AN EXCITED POPULACE THAT HE DIED AT HINDLEY HALL,
THE SEAT OF HIS ELDEST AND ONLY SURVIVING BROTHER, SIR ROBERT HOLT LEIGH, BAR[T].
MAY 13TH 1831, AGED 52 YEARS.
AS A MEMORIAL OF THEIR HIGH ESTEEM,
AND IN ADMIRATION OF HIS INFLEXIBLE PUBLIC INTEGRITY AND PRIVATE WORTH,
HIS NUMEROUS FRIENDS HAVE CAUSED THIS MONUMENT TO BE ERECTED.
M[R]. LEIGH'S REMAINS WERE INTERRED IN THE FAMILY VAULT AT UP HOLLAND ABBEY CHURCH,
IN THE COUNTY OF LANCASTER.

THIS LARGE MURAL monument is carved in high relief from white First Statuary Carrara marble. At its top is a pediment containing a carved crest (a demi-lion rampant, holding in the paws a lozenge charged with a rose of York and Lancaster);[211] below this is a scroll with the motto 'IN HOC SIGNO VINCES'. A carved portrait figure of Robert Holt Leigh occupies the area under the pediment. It depicts a seated figure, dressed in robes, holding a folio open on his knee. The date 1688 appears, carved in low relief, on the pages of the book. The inscription tablet, of Second Statuary grey-veined Carrara marble is set under the effigy. It is 40.6 cm (h) by 116.9 cm (w) and is supported by two plain brackets. The words 'SCULPTOR:- R. WESTMACOTT, JUN. WILTON PLACE, LONDON' are carved to the right of the tablet.

This monument to Roger Holt Leigh was raised by public subscription. Richard Westmacott the Younger (1799–1872), the son of one of the leading sculptors of the day, was given the commission. The posthumous portrait presented the sculptor with some difficulties, but despite this the monument was judged by the local press as an excellent work of art: 'The likeness, considering that the artist had to work from a miniature and a pencil drawing, the former taken many years ago, is good: but there is too much hair on the head, and the countenance is more juvenile than that of the respected deceased'.[212]

BECKETT, CHRISTOPHER

Lady Chapel, Wa.T. 54 (North Wall)

In Memory of **CHRISTOPHER BECKETT** of Meanwood Esquire
A Justice of the Peace, and Deputy Lieutenant of the West Riding,
twice mayor of Leeds.
Born xxvi[th] January mdcclxxvii, he died at Torquay xv[th] March mdcccxlvii,
and was interred in the adjacent Vault.
He was an active Magistrate, a faithful Dispenser of
Public Trusts, and a liberal Supporter of the Calls of
Religion and the Claims of Charity ☦

THIS RECTANGULAR fine-grained sandstone tablet is 54.2 cm (h) by 175 cm (w). The carved inscription is coloured so the upper case letters are filled with red and the lower case letters are black. It is all that remains of an elaborate Caen stone canopied monument carved by R. Mawer of Leeds, to a design by the town architect, a Mr Dobson.[213] It was commissioned by Christopher Beckett's surviving brothers and sisters at an overall cost of £436 15s. 7d., which included iron rails set around it at £8 10s. 10d. and the memorial window above (by W. Wailes of Newcastle) at £45. The original monument was 12 feet, 10 inches high by 11 feet 3 inches wide and projected three feet from the wall. It had a cusped arch with massive angle buttresses and was decorated with pinnacles and angels holding scrolls. The interior was worked in diaper and a shield with the Beckett arms was in its centre.[214] It was dismantled, after approval was obtained from the family,[215] to make way for the gilded oak reredos installed in the Lady Chapel when it was dedicated as a memorial chapel in 1922. Only the central slab containing the details of Christopher Beckett's life and death was retained from the original memorial and set in its present position in the wall. The rest of the monument is in the church hall.

Christopher Beckett was the second son of Sir John Beckett (q.v.). He was a banker and was mayor of Leeds in 1819, and 1829. He lived at Meanwood Hall and died unmarried.[216]

BECKETT, SIR JOHN

Lady Chapel, Wa.T. 55 (North Wall)

THE INSCRIPTION TABLETS of this large mural monument are carved from white First Statuary Carrara marble and are set on magnesian limestone plates. These are flanked by grey-veined Carrara marble surrounds. The whole rests on a black painted medium-grained sandstone sill and ground with an angular top. The Beckett coat of arms (gules, a fesse between three boars' heads couped erminois) and crest (a boar's head couped or, pierced by a cross patée fichée erect sable)[217] are applied to upper area of the pyramidal ground. The motto 'PRODESSE CIVIBUS' is contained, with the arms and crest, within a wreath of palm leaves. A heavy pediment is set over the upper inscription tablet for Sir John. The tablet is flanked by scrolls and set above carved drapery, with fluted columns below. That for Lady Beckett is set into a lower frame flanked by fluted columns and resting on the protruding black shelf. The letters of the inscriptions are incised and filled with black, some of which is missing.

In the early eighteenth century two brothers of the Beckett family moved from Barnsley to Leeds and became woollen merchants. They were successful in their enterprise and persuaded local business friends to join them in chartering a vessel to export local goods to Portugal and to import Portuguese produce, especially wine. Again, this was successful and the foreign currency exchanges this venture required gradually supplanted the actual woollen business, which was left to others. John Beckett became a partner in the first bank to be established in Leeds, Lodge and Arthington. The Becketts then became the leading banking family in the town.[218]

TURNER, JAMES KING

Lady Chapel, M.S. 14

THIS MONUMENT slab, possibly limestone, is 182.8 cm (l) and 99.6 cm (w).

Alexander Turner had been mayor of Leeds in 1793 and 1810.[235]

IN Memory of JAMES KING TURNER
Son of MR ALEXR TURNER
in this Town Merchant, who died 14th
of Auguſt *1790*, aged 3 years.
Also the Body of the above mentioned
ALEXANDER TURNER Esqr
Alderman of this *Borough*;
who died the 24th of July 1816,
aged 63 Years.

BECKETT, CHRISTOPHER

Lady Chapel, M.S. 15

THIS FINE-GRAINED sandstone monument slab is 90.3 cm (l) and 182.6 cm (w).

CHRISTOPHER BECKETT

DIED 15TH MARCH 1847.

PRESTON, WILLIAM

Lady Chapel, M.S. 16

THIS FINE-GRAINED sandstone monument slab is 181.5 cm (l) by 99 cm (w). Its surface has been damaged and some of its inscription lost.

Beneath are depoſited
The Remains of WILLIAM PRESTON
who died April 7th 1801
aged *27* Years.
Alſo of
The Revd   PRESTON
who died Dec.
aged _ years
Son of HENRY PRESTON of this Town
Who also was interred

Alſo the remains of the above
HENRY PRESTON Eſq
who died Dec 20. 1808 Aged 71 years

Alſo of ANN Relict of the above
HENRY PRESTON Eſqr
who died *at Doncaster* on the
of December 1824 aged 68 Years
AND WAS BURIED IN THIS VAULT

ARMISTEAD, THOMAS

Lady Chapel, M.S. 17

Tho Armiſtead who departed
this life 21. of Aug. 1767 aged__
Also the Body of the above
Tho Armiſtead who
departed this life July 16.
aged 68 Years

THIS MONUMENT slab (possibly lime-stone), which is 180 cm (l) by 95 cm (w), is worn and the inscription is difficult to decipher.

Thomas Armistead the younger, according to the *Parish Register of Burials*, died of consumption. He was the son of Thomas Armistead of Little Woodhouse.

COOKSON, WILLIAM

Lady Chapel, M.S. 18

WILLIAM COOKSON ESQ. of LEEDS
who for a long courſe of Years
diſcharged in an active and
exemplary manner the duties of
a Magiſtrate and of many other
important truſts committed to
his Charge. He died July 22 A D
1743 aged 74 Years.
Likewiſe SUSANNA his Wife
Daughter of MICHAEL IDLE ESQ.
of Leeds who died Feb 12th A D
1740 aged 61 Years.
Alſo Mr. THOMAS COOKSON Merch't
their ſecond Son, who receded
From Publick Employment that
he might with more leisure,
cultivate every Virtue which can
adorn a private life. He died 20
Aug. A D 1773 aged 65 Years
Alſo of Mrs ELISABETH COOKSON
their Daughter who died 23rd Octr.
A.D. 1781 aged 70 Years

Alſo Margaret, Relict of the
above THOMAS COOKSON, ~~ who died
Oct 24th 1803 aged 82Years
Alſo WILL. COOKSON ESQ. late Alderman
of this Borough, Son of the above
WILLIAM COOKSON who died Feb 1 1811, Aged 61

THIS EGGLESTONE marble monument slab, which is very worn, is 180 cm (l) by 96 cm (w). When the new church was built it was in the floor of the north tower and was moved to its present position in the 1990s. Its inscription has been partially reconstructed from Rusby's transcription[236] and checked against the parish registers.

Willliam Cookson had a colourful past having been imprisoned in Newgate in 1715 for his supposed Jacobite sympathies. Despite this he merited a warm tribute in the *Parish Register of Burials* at the time of his death: 'He was thrice Mayor of this Corporation, of which he was the greatest Ornament. His virtues shined with an amiable Lustre thro' the various Scenes of Life. He was a pious Christian, a generous Benefactor, an honest Tradesman, a tender Husband, an indulgent Parent, a sincere Friend, and complete Gentleman.' His wife, Susanna, was the daughter of Michael Idle (q.v.), mayor of Leeds in 1690.[237] He was in business with his younger brother Samuel, was a colleague of William Milner (q.v.) on the Pious Uses Committee, and was himself mayor of Leeds in 1712, 1735 and 1758.[238]

William's second son Thomas was elected to the Corporation in 1742 but resigned in 1744 and retired from public life. William's grandson, however, also William, was mayor in 1783 and 1801. He married Mary, the daughter of Henry Scott, Esq., (mayor of Leeds 1748) and was a friend of William Wilberforce, was a prominent Church and King advocate in the West Riding, and was a magistrate in both the county and in Leeds. His eventual death in 1811 was caused by 'the sudden intelligence of the rascality of his partner or agent in America.' His son Francis Thomas (1786–1859) was the incumbent of St John's at the age of twenty-four.[239]

CRIMEAN WAR MEMORIAL
North Tower, Wa.T. 8 (West Wall)

IN MEMORY OF
LIEUT. JAMES MARSHALL,
68 TH. REGT. L.I.,
THE NON-COMMISSIONED OFFICERS
AND PRIVATES, NATIVES OF LEEDS,
WHO DIED FOR THEIR COUNTRY
IN THE CRIMEAN WAR
FROM 1854 TO 1856.

PRIVATE	JAMES GREENWELL	ABM	KEIGHLEY BRAMHAM
	GEORGE LANGWORTHY		FREDERICK DIXON
	THOMAS LEVITT		JESSE HARGREAVES
	JOSEPH MERRITT		BENJAMIN JAGGER
	THOMAS PARKER		JOHN ROBINSON
	CHARLES PEAT		JAMES SWALES
	THOMAS PRATT		LAWRENCE STEEL
	JOHN RILEY		WILLIAM TODD
	JOHN SIMMONS		13TH REGIMENT L.I.
	GEORGE SWALES	PRIVATE	CHARLES BLAKEY
	JOSEPH SMITH		21ST ROYAL N.B. FUSILIERS
	CHARLES FOLLEY	PRIVATE	JOHN WARD
	CHARLES WARD		33RD REGIMENT
	ISAAC WALTON	PRIVATE	TIMOTHY HOLROYD
	88TH REGIMENT		WILLIAM SHACKLETON
SERGEANT	JAMES MATTHEWMAN		34TH REGIMENT
	95TH REGIMENT	PRIVATE	JOHN PARKER
PRIVATE	JAMES PICKLES		44TH REGIMENT
	97TH REGIMENT	PRIVATE	CHARLES EMMETT
PRIVATE	ROBERT TURTON		WILLIAM NICHOLSON
	ALFRED ELSWORTH		WILLIAM ROBERTS
	SAPPER & MINERS		ELI WOOD
PRIVATE	JOHN HEATON		50TH REGIMENT
	LAND TRANSPORT SERVICE	PRIVATE	JOHN MITCHELL
	GEORGE VAREY		55TH REGIMENT
	5TH DRAGOON GUARDS	PRIVATE	JOSEPH SIMPSON
PRIVATE	JOHN TURNBULL		68TH LIGHT INFANTRY
	VIII HUSSARS	SERGEANT	WILLIAM BLYTHE
SERGEANT	JOHN MACAULEY	CORPORAL	JAMES THACKRAY
	13TH LIGHT DRAGOONS	PRIVATE	ISAAC ABBOTT
PRIVATE	JOHN MURPHY		THOMAS ABBOTT
	SCOTS FUSILIER GUARDS		WILLIAM ANDERSON
PRIVATE	JOHN SMITH		BENJAMIN BECK
	7TH ROYAL FUSILIERS		ROBERT FOSSEY
CORPORAL	WILLIAM HARGREAVES		GEORGE FOSTER
PRIVATE	DAVID ASQUITH		JOHN FRANCE
	ROBERT BATES		THOMAS FLETCHER
	WILLIAM BEAUMONT		

T HIS RECTANGULAR white marble mural monument is made up of four panels of white Carrara marble. The monument overall is 193.7 cm (h) by 41.1 cm (w). The incised lettering is coloured black.

This is all that remains of a substantial monument by Dennis, Lee and Welsh, of Woodhouse Lane, Leeds that was erected by public subscription and dedicated 23 June 1859. The description from the *Leeds Intelligencer* at the time of the dedication indicates how impressive it was:

> [with a] ... pedestal enclosing a panel of white Statuary marble, with a canopy of a gothic design in harmony with the architecture of the Church. Upon the pedestal is placed a sculptured group, consisting of two life-sized figures – a dying soldier with the Angel of Victory placing upon his head a wreath. The rocky ground appears strewed with the wreck and spoil of war. The canopy over the table, on which is inscribed the names of the gallant heroes whose names it is intended to perpetuate, consists of a groined and foliated series of trefoiled flying arches. The cusps of which have angels recording in open books the acts of the heroes. On each pilaster are inscribed the names of the victories in the Crimea [Alma, Balaklava, Inkermann and Sebastopol], entwined with laurel ... The height of the monument is 14′, and it has taken about 15 tons of material for its a construction ... The cost of the memorial is about 300 guineas, and about half the amount has yet to be obtained.[248]

Dennis, Welsh and Lee were evidently so proud of the monument that they used illustrations of it in their advertisements for some years after its installation.[249]

The monument was dismantled following a Parish Church Council report 21 January 1952, which dealt with the cramped conditions obtaining in the north porch after a new inner screen (now removed) had been erected. The report concluded that, after inspection, the Michael Sadler memorial was fit to be moved but the Durham Light Infantry (DLI) Crimean Memorial was showing signs of decay and could not be moved. It was therefore decided that the Sadler memorial be removed and a new position found for it at the University of Leeds (in St George's Fields, where it remains), away from the church altogether, but that DLI memorial should be destroyed, apart from the memorial tablets, which would be set in the wall behind the original sites of the monuments. The memorial was accordingly broken up and the pieces buried in the churchyard. The two Crimean War flags were returned to the DLI headquarters.[250]

William Milner

JACKSON, FABER

North Tower, Wa.T. 15 (East Wall)

THE INSCRIPTION OF this sandstone monument is framed by a black semi-circular arch, which rests on a pair of plain-shafted columns with Corinthian capitals. The incised letters of the inscription are infilled with black. A cherub's head flanked by outstretched wings is carved in each of the two upper corners of the monument. Thoresby referred to this monument in the *Ducatus*[266] but described it as being made of painted wood and fixed to a pillar in the high choir.

*A*djacent
*L*ieth interred
the body of faber
*J*ackson Son of M[R].
*J*ohn Jackson
of Simpsonfold in
*L*eeds who departed
THis life the 14TH of
APRIL *A*nno: 1681
*AL*so HAИИAH Mother
TO THE AFORESAID Faber
WHO DIED Y[e] 20th OF ИOVEMB[R]
AИ°. 1700. Ætatis Suæ 47
Also THO, Son to Y[e] Afore
said Hannah WHO DIeD
JULY THe 21 - 1706
AGed 29 Year.

MIDGLEY, ISABELLA
North Tower, Wa.T. 16 (East Wall)

Here under is intered the mortal
remaines of Iſabella the dearly beloved
wife of Robt. Midgley Chirurgion
daughter of George Neale M.D.
whoſe vertues She truely imitated
She died the 17th of Feb. 1706
after a Godly, Righteus, & Sober
life of two and forty years to
whoſe memory her diſconſolate
Huſband plac't this: Also Near
this PLace is Interred the saiD
Robert Midgley Gent.who aF-
ter a Usefull Charitable &
Pious LiFE OF 70 Years
Departed October 16:1723

THE LETTERS OF this mural monument
are carved onto a black-painted sandstone
inscription tablet so the letters, the colour of the
natural stone, stand out in contrast to the black
ground. The inscription tablet itself is contained in a stele-shaped frame of carved Second
Statuary Carrara marble. The sides of the frame
contain carved hanging garlands of flowers and
foliage. The curved apron below the inscription
tablet is separated from the tablet by a moulded sill and terminates in a carved foliate pendant at the bottom centre.

The Midgley family originally came from
Midgley near Halifax. Isabella's father was a
doctor in Leeds who in 1682 lived near the Bear
Inn, Briggate. Her husband, Robert, also set up
as a surgeon in Briggate.[267] According to the
Parish Register of Burials 'Mrs Isabella, the wife
of Mr Robt Midgley of Briggatte' was buried on
20 February 1706/7.

FEARN, THOMAS

City of Leeds Room, Wa.T. 6 (North Wall)

This RECTANGULAR brass tablet is 36 cm (h) by 50.9 cm (w). The engraved lettering is very worn, and the inscription has been reconstructed with the aid of Rusby's transcription and the parish registers.[272] The tablet is undecorated apart from the four chevrons engraved before the word 'ALSO' in the fifth line.

The Fearnes had been residents of Leeds from at least the sixteenth century with many records in the early parish registers. The Nether Milns was a large mill complex that was probably medieval in origin although, it was outside the manorial boundary. The first documentary reference to it is in 1636.[273] It entered the Fearne family holdings *c.* 1720, through marriage with the Dunwell family.[274] The Nether Milns were set up on Fearne's Island where the Timble (Sheepscar) Beck joined the river Aire, just by the great weir at Crown Point.

There is a reference in the *Parish Register of Baptisms* of 1725 to Thomas, Mr Josiah Fearne's child, 'of the Cross', born on June 8. This may refer to the same Josiah Fearne, salter and one of the lords of the manor, who was hanged on 25 March 1749 in York, for the murder of one Thomas Grave; an infamous case, which earned an extraordinarily condemnatory entry in the parish register for that year: 'This probably is the First Lord of the Manor of Leedes that made his Exit at the Gallows and God Grant he may be the last. Fearne's Temper was extremely rigid to the Poor and his Dependents, that he was dreaded by All, but beloved by None.' Josiah Fearne was the brother-in-law of Thomas Dunwell.[275]

The parish register of 1750 recorded the baptism of Thomas, the child of Mr Thomas Fearne of the Bank, born on 30 October. Also in 1803 is recorded the death from jaundice of 'John Fearn', married man of Nether Mills, who died aged fifty-two years, and was buried on 8 August 1803.

INTERR'D IS HERE THE BODY OF
M[R] THO[S] FEARN S[ALTER]
NETHER MILNS [LEEDS WHO] DIED THE
13TH OF NOV[R] AD   1758 AGED —
««ALSO
THE BODY OF M[R THOMAS FEARN]
ATTORNEY AT LAW, [SON OF THE]
SAID THO[S] FEARNE WHO DEPARTED
THIS LIFE THE 2[D] D[AY OF NOV 1774]
AGED [24] YEARS
ALSO
JN[O] FEARNE SON OF THE ABOVE
THO[S] FEARNE OF LEEDS DRY
SALTER WHO DEPARTED THIS
LIFE AUG: 6th. 1803 AGED 52 YEARS
ALSO
JANE, RELICT OF THE ABOVE
JN[O]. FEARNE DEPARTED THIS LIFE
NOV[R]: 15TH: *1825* AGED 70 YEARS

SMITHSON, MARGARITA

City of Leeds Room, Wa.T. 7 (North Wall)

Alſo. Here lies the body of Mʳˢ Margarita
the Wife of Mʳ. Henry Smithſon, who
departed this life the 19ᵗʰ Febʸ 1793
aged 68 Years.
Also the Body of the above named
Mʳ. Henry Smithſon, who departed this
life the 14ᵗʰ of March 1798, aged 82.

This RECTANGULAR brass tablet is 18.2
cm (h) by 37.8 cm (w). It is undecorated.

Henry Smithson 'the son of the worthy and
facetious Mr. John Smithson, an eminent and
wealthy salter'[276] founded a firm that was
amongst the largest export houses in Leeds during the latter half of the eighteenth century.[277]

IBBITSON, JAMES

City of Leeds Room, Wa.T. 8 (North Wall)

HERE LYETH BVRIED THE
BODY OF IAMES IBBIT~
SON LATE OF LEEDS
KIRKGATE WHO DEPART~
ED THIS LIFE THE 6ᵗʰ OF
IANVARY *1672*
ÆTATIS SVÆ 47

This SHIELD-SHAPED brass tablet is 24.5
cm (h) by 23.8 cm (w). It is undecorated.

According to the *Parish Register of Burials* Mr
James Ibbotson of Kirkgate was buried in
January 1672/3.

BEAVOT, WILLIAM
City of Leeds Room, Wa.T. 22 (Window Sills)

This broad, rectangular brass tablet is 15.5 cm (h) by 28.5 cm (w). It has rounded lower corners and scrolls are engraved at each end of the line 'ANNO DOMINE 1660'.

Susan, the widow of William Beavot of Briggate, Leeds, remarried after his death. Her second husband was James Moxon (q.v.), alderman and mayor of Leeds in 1650.[287]

HERE LYETH BVRIED THE BODY
OF WILLIAM BEAVOT OF LEEDS
WHO DEPARTED THIS LIFE
THE 10TH DAY OF AVGVST
~ANNO DOMINI 1660~
MORS MIHI LVCRVM

SYKES, RICHARD
City of Leeds Room, Wa.T. 23 (Window Sills)

This rectangular brass tablet is 12 cm (h) by 33 cm (w). The fourth and fifth lines of the inscription are decorated with engraved scrollwork. This inscription tablet set on 'large new marble',[288] originally marked the place of burial of Sykes and his wife in the old church.

Richard Sykes was one of three sons of Richard Sykes of Kirkgate, clothier, and his wife Sibell. On the death of his elder brother he inherited the family land holdings at Knowstrop becoming, through marriage (to Elizabeth Mawson), inheritance and purchase, one of the principal land-owners in the burough. He was principal burgess in the years 1629–30 and 1636–37 and is believed to have been the 'first private gentleman in Leeds' to own his own carriage. He died on 27 March 1645 in his burgess house in Briggate during a severe outbreak of plague; Elizabeth having died in August 1644. They had four sons, two of whom died without issue, and one daughter. His grandson, Samuel, was mayor of Leeds in 1674–75. His great-granddaughter Anna was married to Ralph Thoresby and the family of Sykes of Sledmere is also descended from him.[289]

HERE LYETH INTERRED THE BODY
OF THE WOR RICHARD SYKES ALDERMAN
OF LEEDS WHO DEPARTED THIS LIFE
THE 27TH DAY OF MARCH ~o~
~o~ANNO DOMINI 1645~§~
ÃND THE BODY OF ELISABETH HIS WIFE:
WHO EXPYRED SOME MONTHS BEFORE:

LEVER, ANNA
City of Leeds Room, Wa.T. 24 (Window Sills)

ALSO
ANNA THE DAUGHTER AND HEIR
OF THOMAS LEVER OF CHAMBER
IN THE COUNTY OF LANCASTER ESQ.
WIDOW OF THE ABOVENAMED
CHRISTOPHER LOCKWOOD;
AND AFTERWARDS OF
JONATHAN BLACKBURNE OF ORFORD
IN THE SAID COUNTY OF LANCASTER ESQ
DEPARTED THIS LIFE
THE 20THOF SEPTEMBER 1732
AGED 77 YEARS.

THIS BRASS INSCRIPTION tablet is 21.3 cm (h) by 33.5 cm (w). The lettering is raised and contained within a decorated cartouche, which itself is surrounded by raised, embossed scrollwork.

LODGE, RICHARD
City of Leeds Room, Wa.T. 25 (Window Sills)

Ab ingenuis oriundi,
Bonis omnibus chari,
Alterutrorum vero
Amantiſsimi,
Hic sepulti jacent:
Dr Ricardus Lodge
et
Uxor ejus Elisabetha
Amabilis
Hæc obiit VIII° *die Maii* 1731
llle XXVI° *Novembris 1749.*
Qui ſtirpem perantiquam.
Antiquis moribus, honestavit
Et omnia sibi post putavit eſsi
Pro hoc Elogio

THIS BRASS TABLET is 46.3 cm (h) by 31 cm (w). Its engraved inscription is very worn but remnants of engraved armorials are faintly visible. The arms of the Lodge family were: per fesse gules and sable, a lion rampant argent, semée of cross-crosslets of the first.[290]

Dr Richard Lodge and his wife lived in Call Lane.[291]

CHARLES[WORTH], ANN

City of Leeds Room, M.S. 1

THIS STONE MONUMENT slab was uncovered during the 2001 renovations of the City of Leeds Room. It had previously been covered with screed and carpet. After the inscription was noted, the floor was re-covered and the monument hidden. The surface of the stone was damaged and the inscription was difficult to read.

The inscription has been partially reconstructed from the entry for Ann Charlesworth in the *Parish Register of Burials*: Ann, the daughter of Mr John Charlesworth of Albion Street died of 'Water in Brain' aged two years and was buried on 30 May 1810. She is also commemorated in the large mural memorial for her father, John Beedam Charlesworth (q.v.).

IN MEMORY —-
ANN, Daughter of J[OHN]
and ANN CHARLES[WORTH]
——-n who died —-[May]
1810, aged [2 Years]
[and] of WILLIAM, their Son
died *the 25th* of October——-
aged 40 Years
Also JOHN their Son who died
on the 23rd of December 1846
aged 43 Years.

O NEIL, CRISTIANA

City of Leeds Room, M.S. 2

THIS STONE MONUMENT slab was uncovered during the 2001 renovations of the City of Leeds Room. It had previously been covered with screed and carpet. After the inscription was noted, the floor was re-covered and the monument hidden. The surface of the stone was damaged and much of the inscription has been lost. It has been reconstructed from Rusby's transcription.[300]

IN MEMORY [OF]
CRISTIANA SAWER, [WIFE OF]
JOHN O NEIL, *of Lond*[*on, who*]
[d]eparted this life March 10.[1826]
aged 38 Years.
Also CRISTIANA, Relict [of the]
[late] JOSEPH FIGAR[I of this]
Town and Mother of the
Cristiana Sawer O [Neil]
who departed this Life [Jan'y]
1812, aged 84 Years
Also of MARGARET 3 D[aughter]
of the above named [John and]
CRISTIANA O neil, who [departed]
this Life the 16th of M[ay 18—]
ALSO CLARA, WIFE OF JOH[N WALSH]
AND DAUGHTER OF THE AB[OVE NAMED]
JOHN O NEIL, WHO DIED [FEBRUARY]
1852, AGED 34 YEA[RS]

KITSON CLARK, EDWIN

Gallery, Wa.T. 1 (South East Pew)

EDWIN KITSON CLARK died 1943
for 25 years Warden of this Church
owner & occupier of this pew
where he constantly worshipped as he lived
in humble faith in God's mercy through Christ
& in perfect charity with all men

THIS BRASS TABLET is 8.8 cm (h) by 22.8 cm (w). It is undecorated.

ATKINSON, MILES

Gallery, Wa.T. 2 (West Wall)

A MOULDED CORNICE tops the rectangular inscription tablet of this mural monument. A sarcophagus with opened gadroon-edged lid and paw feet rests on the cornice. A closed mourning urn is set on the lid of the sarcophagus. It is decorated with swags held by rings, carved beading and acanthus leaves, with a carved finial at its apex. Carved brackets at the lower corners support the inscription tablet. The brackets contain deeply carved four-petal flowers and are set above carved scrolls. A carved panel separates the brackets and is decorated with five stylized acanthus leaves, all carved in high relief. The letters of the incised inscription are coloured black.

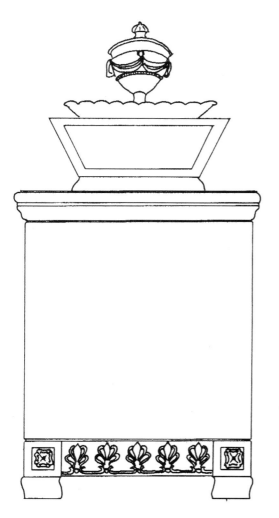

IN A VAULT UNDERNEATH
ARE DEPOSITED THE REMAINS OF
THE REVEREND MILES ATKINSON, B.A.
LECTURER DURING 40 YEARS OF THE PARISH CHURCH OF LEEDS,
VICAR OF KIPPAX,
AND MINISTER OF THIS CHURCH;
WHO DIED 6 FEB^Y 1811,
AGED 70 YEARS.
HIS PUBLIC MINISTRATION WAS MARKED BY
UNWEARIED ZEAL AND PERSEVERING FAITHFULNESS.
ATTENDED THROUGH THE DIVINE BLESSING WITH EXTENSIVE SUCCESS:
HIS FAMILIAR INTERCOURSE,
SUBSERVIENT TO THE SAME RESULT,
WAS DISTINGUISHED BY
UNYIELDING CONSTANCY AND UNABATED TENDERNESS.

ERECTED AT HIS OWN CHARGE THIS *EDIFICE,* STANDS
A MONUMENT
OF HIS LOVE FOR THE SOULS OF MEN,
AND OF HIS FAITH AND HOPE IN THAT SAVIOUR
WHOSE GLORY HE WAS ANXIOUS TO PROMOTE.

A NUMBER OF HIS SURVIVING HEARERS AND FRIENDS
HAVE DEDICATED TO HIS MEMORY
THIS *TOKEN*
OF ESTEEM AND AFFECTION.

I determined not to know any thing among you
save *JESUS CHRIST* and him crucified.
REMOVED FROM S^T PAULS CHURCH 1905.

The Revd Miles Atkinson, the founder of St Paul's Church, Leeds, was the son of the Revd Christopher Atkinson of Thorpe Arch who married Miss Mary Kenion in April 1768. Miles was a celebrated preacher in his time and, as the fashionable residential centre of Leeds moved west, he attracted a large congregation to the new church.[301] He died aged seventy (according to the *Parish Register of Burials,* of a diseased liver) and it was reported afterwards in the *Leeds Intelligencer* that his third son, having travelled over from Manchester for the funeral, caught typhus during his visit to Leeds and only survived his father by two weeks.[302]

St Paul's Church, Park Square was demolished 1905. The art deco National Rivers Authority building now stands in its place in Park Square.[303]

LUPTON, FRANCIS

Gallery, Wa.T. 3 (West Wall)

In the Aisle
Near this place is interred the
Body of FRANCIS LUPTON, who
died *A.D 1717*. Aged *59*:
Also ESTHER his Wife, who died
A D 1726. Aged *57*:
Also WILLIAM. Son of the above
Francis and Esther, who died
March 3rd *1771*. Aged *70*:
And MARY his Wife, who died
Decr 28th *1760*. Aged 45:
Also the Revd WILLM LUPTON, M:A.
Son of the above William and Mary,
who died Feby 3rd *1782* Aged 49:
Also SARAH, Widow of Francis
Lupton, late of Lisbon, Merchant, Son
of the above William and Mary, who
died March 9th 1802. Aged 66:
Also HENRY Son of the above Francis
and Sarah, who died May 22nd *1796*.
Aged 33:

Also ARTHUR, Son of the above
William and Mary Lupton, who died
July 7th *1807*, Aged 59:
And OLIVE, his Wife, who died
April 24th 1803, Aged 49:
Also WILLIAM, Son of the above
Arthur and Olive Lupton who died
August 19th 1828, Aged 51.
Also WILLIAM Son of the above William
Lupton, who died May 23rd 1821 Aged 10.

THIS BRASS TABLET, 55 cm (h) by 24.2 cm (w), is mounted on a wooden plaque.

The Lupton family was one of the most influential in Leeds in the nineteenth and early twentieth centuries. Francis Lupton, the founder of the dynasty, married Esther Midgley of Breary at Adel in 1688. Six years later he was appointed clerk and registrar of the parish church at Leeds. He retained the post until his death in August 1717.[304]

One of his sons, William, was described as a yeoman in his will. A clothier/farmer of Whitkirk, he had business connections with Germany and the Netherlands and had close connections with the cloth firm of a Dutch merchant, Koster, who had settled in Leeds. He was Koster's executor in 1670 and eventually took over his business. William sent his eldest son, Francis, to Portugal as a merchant in 1752. Francis died there following various reverses due firstly to the Lisbon earthquake of 1755, followed by a fire in the customs house in 1764 in which he lost £1500 worth of goods. After his death his wife, Sarah, sent the children to England for their education.

William's second son, William, was the curate of Leeds Parish Church in 1759, and later went Somerset to become the rector of Blagdon. By the time he died he was the curate in charge at Headingley.

William's third son, Arthur, was born in 1748 and was sent at age fifteen to Frankfurt. In 1773 he married Olive, the daughter of David Rider, a well-to-do clothworker who had considerable property in the Leylands and Mabgate. It was regarded as an excellent match: the *Leeds Intelligencer* noted her dowry was £5000. By 1790 the business had become known as Lupton & Co. Merchants, Leylands.

In 1803 Arthur's son William married Ann Darnton, the daughter of a tobacco merchant who lived on the Headrow. After her husband's death in 1828 she carried on the business with her sons Darnton and Arthur, then twenty-two and nineteen. She retired to Gledhow Mount in Harehills Lane in 1858 where she died in 1865.

LUPTON, JOSEPH

Gallery, Wa. T. 4 (West Wall)

THE BRASS INSCRIPTION tablet of this mural monument is set on a wooden plaque. A border, 0.2 cm wide, and set 0.2 cm from the outside edges, surrounds the inscription. A lower area 9.2 cm (h) and 24 cm (w) is bounded by a black border and decorated with a black scrolled motif. Overall, the tablet is 55.1 cm (h) by 24 cm (w).

Also JOSEPH, Son of
the aforesaid William Lupton,
Born January 15th 1816.
Died January 17th 1894.

Also JANE, Widow of
the aforesaid Arthur Lupton,
Born June 7th 1828.
Died May 10th 1900.

Also ELIZA, Widow of
the aforesaid Joseph Lupton,
Born April 4th 1818.
Died November 21st 1901.

Also ANNE, Daughter of
the aforesaid William Lupton,
Born March 1st 1812.
Married Thomas Michael Greenhow, M.D. of
Newcastle-on-Tyne. May 31st 1854.
Died April 8th 1905.

Also MARY, Widow of
the aforesaid John Lupton,
Born November 18th 1828.
Died May 29th 1914.

the early days of the Leeds medical community and the Leeds General Infirmary, see S. T. Anning, *The History of Medicine in Leeds* (Leeds, 1980).

104 Rusby, p. 171.
105 Ibid., p. 165; Thoresby, *Ducatus*, p. 43.
106 Thoresby, *Diaries,* I, 290.
107 Thoresby, *Ducatus*, p. 45.
108 Ibid., p. 184; WYASL, PCA, P68.
109 Kirby, 'Aldermen'.
110 Taylor, pp. 107–08.
111 WYASL, PCA, P68.
112 Thoresby, *Diaries,* II, 180.
113 Wilson, p. 22.
114 Rusby, p. 213.
115 Ibid., pp. 226–27.
116 Wilson, p. 31.
117 Rusby, pp. 186–87.
118 Thoresby, *Ducatus*, p. 45.
119 Ibid., p. 52; Rusby, p. 176.
120 Thoresby, *Ducatus*, p. 48; Rusby, pp. 133–34.
121 Rusby, p. 238.
122 Wilson, p. 76.
123 Wilson, p. 76; Taylor, pp. 168–69.
124 Thoresby, *Ducatus*, p. 51; Rusby, pp. 138–39.
125 Brooke, 309.
126 Rusby, p. 192.
127 Ibid., p. 192; Brooke, 309.
128 Rusby, p. 224.
129 Thoresby, *Ducatus*, p. 44; Rusby, p. 147.
130 Rusby, p. 202.
131 Ibid., p. 203.
132 WYASL, PCA, P68.
133 Rusby, p. 202.
134 Ibid., p. 222.
135 Ibid., p. 34.
136 *LI*, 6 Apr. 1756.
137 WYASL, PCA, P68.
138 *LI*, 17 Nov. 1800.
139 Rusby, p. 222.
140 Ibid., p. 208.
141 Ibid., p. 173; Wilson, p. 32.
142 *LI*, 8 Feb. 1763.
143 Rusby, p. 223.
144 Ibid., p. 201.
145 Ibid., p. 199.
146 Thoresby, *Ducatus*, p. 54.
147 Rusby, p. 243.

LADY CHAPEL WALLS

148 Rusby, p. 225.
149 According to the *Parish Register of Burials* the elder Samuel Predam died aged sixty-five years 16 Nov. 1795 after a 'lingering illness'. See WYASL, PCA, P68.
150 On 25 May 1801, nearly two months after the letter had been written.
151 *LM*, 16 Jan. 1802; Rusby, p. 225.
152 Wilson, p. 25.
153 S. Wrathmell, *Pevsner Architectural Guide: Leeds* (Yale, 2005), pp.14, 205.
154 See E. Hargrave, 'The Leeds Volunteers 1794 to 1802', *PThS*, XXVIII (1928), 265–84, for an account of the Leeds Volunteer Corps.
155 'At a meeting of the Old Volunteers and others, friends and admirers of Col. Lloyd, … Mr. Alderman Hall moved that a monument be erected for the purpose of showing respect to that most excellent man … [it was] in the midst of the American War, that Col. Lloyd commenced his military career: a corps of volunteers was then formed for home service at a period when almost all the regular forces of the country were engaged in distant warfare … This corps was of essential service in the preservation of the public peace, which was at that time disturbed by riots on account of the high price of corn. This corps was dissolved at the termination of the American War … the formation of a second corps, in 1794, when this country was engaged with a war with France … This corps, which consisted of three hundred men was commanded by Col. Lloyd'. See *LM*, 26 Apr. 1828; Wrathmell, p. 205; Wilson, p. 25; see also Hargrave *passim*.
156 *LM*, 26 Apr. 1828.
157 WYASL, PCA, P68/46/4.
158 *LM*, 30 May 1812.
159 *LI*, 28 Aug. 1809.
160 Esdaile, *YAJ*, Vol. XXXVI, 78–108, 137–63, 93.
161 *Y(orkshire) P(ost)*, 24 May 1911.
162 WYASL, PCA, P68/46/4; P68/50/34.
163 WYASL, PCA, P68/50/34.
164 Rusby, p. 253.
165 Taken from the churchwardens' minute book, 1910, pp. 74–75. See WYASL, PCA, P68/46/4.
166 Taken from the minutes of the churchwardens' meetings, WYASL, PCA, P68/46/5; P68/46/6. Approval for a memorial brass 25 inches wide and 18 inches deep was granted by the Diocese of Ripon 25 October 1913. WYASL, PCA, P68/50/34.
167 WYASL, PCA, P68/46/5; P68/46/9; P68/50/34.
168 Taylor, pp. 107–08; Rusby, pp. 231-32.
169 *LI,* 20 Feb. 1797.
170 Rusby, p. 232.
171 Pemberton, 54–86.
172 *LM*, 14 May 1796.
173 Thoresby, *Ducatus*, pp. 220, 256; Rusby, p. 166.
174 Wilson, p. 243.
175 *LM*, 15 Aug. 1749.
176 Rusby, p. 167.
177 *LI*, 21 Oct. 1799.
178 *LI,* 30 Sept. 1799.
179 G. D. Lumb, 'John Thoresby', *PThS*, XXII (1915), 55–57.
180 The monument is illustrated in the 1715 edition of the *Ducatus*. In the illustration the pediment is shown with a pair of lions rampant carved at each end of the cornice, each lion holding a battle-axe. No signs of the lions survive on the present monument if, indeed, they were ever present.
181 *YP*, 28 Mar. 1922; *Leeds Parish Church Statement of Accounts, 1922* (1922).
182 Thoresby, *Ducatus*, p. 8.
183 Ibid., p. 48; Rusby, p. 52.
184 Barstow Arms: ermine, upon a fesse cotised sable, three crescents or. Thoresby, *Ducatus*, p. 48; Rusby, p. 151
185 WYASL, PCA, P68/46/5, P68/50/34; *YP*, 2 July 1931.
186 Rusby, p. 156.

187 Ibid., p. 192.

188 Ibid., p. 194.

189 Thoresby, *Ducatus*, pp. 79–80.

190 Gunnis, p. 319.

191 The Roll of Honour in the Side Chapel was discussed at a churchwardens' meeting 1 February 1922 when it was agreed it would be unveiled 28 March 1922. WYASL, PCA, P68/46/5. The ceremony was reported in *YP*, 29 March 1922.

192 'Upon the same Marble, a modern Brass …' Thoresby, *Ducatus*, p. 43.

193 Ibid., p. 67.

194 Kirby, 'Aldermen'.

195 Thoresby, *Ducatus*, p. 50.

196 Rusby, p. 145.

197 Kirby, 'Aldermen'.

198 Thoresby, *Ducatus*, p. 52.

199 Rusby, p. 161.

200 Ibid., p. 251.

201 Taylor, pp. 349–50.

202 Thoresby, *Ducatus*, p. 45; Rusby, pp. 180–81.

203 Rusby, pp. 180–81.

204 Ibid., p.182; Thoresby, *Ducatus*, p. 44.

205 Rusby, p. 182.

206 Ibid., p. 182.

207 Ibid., p. 182.

208 Wilson, p. 15; Kirby, 'Aldermen'.

209 Thoresby, *Diaries*, I, 283.

210 Thoresby, *Ducatus*, p. 43.

211 Rusby, p. 245.

212 *LI*, 18 Oct. 1832.

213 The original monument is illustrated in Rusby, facing p. 249 and in Moore, *Church 1877*, engraving opposite p. 21. Full descriptions are given by Rusby, pp. 234–35 and R. W. Moore, *A History of the Parish Church of Leeds and its Ancient Pillar* (1872), p. 20.

214 The costs of the tomb were borne by Christopher Beckett's surviving brothers and sisters. The costs included those incurred by R. Mawer, for carving, £254 17s. 10d.; W. Wailes of Newcastle for the stained glass memorial window, £45; protective rails, £8 10s. 10d. The architect's charge was £35. The entire costs of tomb were £376 15s. 7d. plus £60 fees. The original costs were estimated at £500. The memorial was 11 feet 3 inches wide, and rose 12 feet 10 inches to the top of the angels. WYASL, PCA, P68/50/4.

215 The churchwardens reported on 16 June 1919 that the Beckett family had approved the removal of the Beckett Tomb from the side chapel to some other place in the church. Taken from the churchwardens' meetings minutes, WYASL, PCA, P68/46/5. The petition to remove the memorial was granted by the Diocese of Ripon 26 Oct. 1921. The memorial was described as that standing in front of the window in the north east corner of the chapel. It was intended to remove it and to place a slab record of his life and death under the new sill of the same window. At the same time the memorial reredos was to be erected and the black and white marble flooring was also to be inserted. Ripon Diocesan Registry Ripon, entered Faculty Book No. 9, p. 164. WYASL, PCA, P68/50/34.

216 Rusby, p. 236; see also Pemberton, 54–86.

217 Rusby, p. 234.

218 Pemberton, 56–57; Taylor, pp. 304–05.

219 Wilson, p. 211.

220 Taylor, p. 304.

LADY CHAPEL FLOOR

221 Rusby, p. 184.

222 Thoresby, *Ducatus*, p. 50.

223 Ibid., p. 212.

224 *LI*, 4 Sept. 1841.

225 Rusby, p. 258.

226 Wilson, p. 22.

227 Pemberton, 68.

228 Rusby, p. 221; Wilson, p. 240.

229 Argent, a boar's head couped, between three crescents sable. Rusby, p. 251.

230 See *LI*, 30 Apr. 1798. Edward Sanderson Tennant, the son of Thomas Tennant, died aged two years, and was buried 22 March 1799. According to the *Parish Register of Burials*, he died of 'Fitts'.

231 Most of the biographical details in this entry covering the lives of Henry Hall and his family are from Brooke, 322–25.

232 Taylor, p. 474.

233 Mr Alderman Hall proposed, at a meeting of the Old Volunteers and friends and admirers of Col. Lloyd, that a monument be erected 'for the purpose of showing respect to that most excellent man'. See *LM*, 26 Apr. 1828.

234 Brooke, 235.

235 Rusby, p. 229; the entry in the *Parish Register of Burials* for 27 July 1816 reads 'One of the Senior Aldermen of this Borough whereof he had twice been the Mayor'. WYASL, PCA, P68.

236 Rusby, p. 204.

237 Susanna, wife of William Cookson, Esq., buried 15 Feb. 1739/40. From the *Parish Register of Burials*, WYASL, PCA, P68.

238 Wilson, p. 242; Friedman, *Architecture*, p. 6.

239 Wilson, p. 242.

NORTH TOWER

240 J. T. Ward, 'The Factory Reform Movement', *PThS*, XLVI (1963), 87–118; WYASL, PCA, P68/50/34.

241 The monument was erected after representations by the Oastler Committee. WYASL, PCA, P68/50/34.

242 The Pawson family was written about extensively by C. B. Norcliffe, 'The Pawson Inventory and Pedigree', *PThS*, IV (1895), 162–68.

243 *LI*, 27 Feb. 1759.

244 Thoresby, *Ducatus*, p. 22; Rusby, p. 149.

245 Thoresby, *Ducatus*, p. 76; Rusby, p. 195.

246 Rusby, p. 196.

247 Wilson, p. 243; Rusby, p. 216.

248 *LI*, 25 June 1859.

249 A copy of an advertisement showing the monument is in research notes *Public Sculpture in Leeds*, held at the Henry Moore Institute Library, Leeds. See Hall.

250 WYASL, PCA, P68/50/34.

251 Rusby, p. 158; Taylor, pp. 150–51; Friedman, *Architecture*, pp. 4–6. William Milner makes many appearances in Ralph Thoresby's *Diaries*.

Hepton, Sir Wilfred Lawrence*	1911	Lady Chapel, Wa.T. 8
Hey, Alice	1794	Nave, M.S. 5
Hey, Dorothy*	1695/6	Altar Flats, M.S. 3
Hey, Elizabeth	1783	Nave, M.S. 5
Hey, John*	1774	Nave, M.S. 5
Hey, Margaret	1706	Altar Flats, M.S. 3
Hey, Mary	1768	Nave, M.S. 6
Hey, Richard	1789	Nave, M.S. 5
Hey, Richard	1740	Nave, M.S. 6
Hey, Richard*	1766	Nave, M.S. 6
Hey, Robert Banks	1774	Nave, M.S. 5
Hey, Samuel	1706	Altar Flats, M.S. 3
Hey, Samuel		Nave M.S. 5
Hicke, Ann*	1661	Lady Chapel, Wa.T. 50
Hicke, John	1673/4	Lady Chapel, Wa.T. 49
Hicke, William	1673	Lady Chapel, Wa.T. 49
Hill, Arthur	1893	West End, Wa.T. 2
Hill, Charles Edward	1878	West End, Wa.T. 2
Hill, Francis Chorley	1902	West End, Wa.T. 2
Hill, John William*	1882	West End, Wa.T. 2
Hippon, Maria	1712	Lady Chapel, Wa.T. 48
Hodgson, Linnhe*	1909	Altar Flats, Column 1, North Side
Hollis, Arthur*	1964	North Aisle, Wa.T. 5
Hook, Walter Farquhar*	1875	Sanctuary, N. Side, Table Monument 1
Hopkinson, Elizabeth*	1755	Nave, M.S. 7
Hopkinson, John		Nave, M.S. 7
Hopkinson?, Martha	17—	Nave, M.S. 7
Hopkinson, Richard		Nave, M.S. 7
Hopkinson?, Robert	1790	Nave Floor, M.S. 7
Horncastle, Elizabeth	1749/50	City of Leeds Room, Wa.T. 14
Horncastle, John*	1737	City of Leeds Room, Wa.T. 14
Horncastle, Richard	1753	City of Leeds Room, Wa.T.14
Horncastle, Thomas	1765	Nave, M.S. 25
Horne, William*	1685	Lady Chapel, Wa.T. 45
Hudson, Arthur Edward*	1887	South Aisle, Wa.T. 14
Ibbetson, Bartholomow*	1676	Nave, M.S. 4
Ibbetson, Catharine	1754	Nave, M.S. 32
Ibbetson, Catharine*	1740	Nave, M.S. 32
Ibbetson, Elizabeth	1751	Nave, M.S. 3
Ibbetson, Elizabeth	1752	Nave, M.S. 32
Ibbetson, George*	1732/3	Nave, M.S. 3
Ibbetson, Isabella	1757	Nave, M.S. 32
Ibbetson, James	1739	Nave, M.S. 3
Ibbetson, Joshua	1700/1	Nave, M.S. 33
Ibbetson, Mary	1715/6	Nave, M.S. 33
Ibbetson, Sir Henry	1761	Nave, M.S. 32
Ibbitson, James*	1672/3	City of Leeds Room, Wa.T. 8
Ibbitson, James*	1661	Nave, M.S. 33
Ibbitson, Mary	1685	Nave, M.S. 33
Idle, Lucy	1708	North Tower, Wa.T. 14
Idle, Michael*	1696/7	North Tower, Wa.T. 14
Ikin, Abel*	1757	Nave, M.S. 55
Ikin, Arthur	1791	Nave, M.S. 55
Ikin, Mary	1791	Nave, M.S. 55
International Year of Disabled People*		South Aisle, Wa.T. 6
Iveson, ?*	1717	Altar Flats, M.S. 16
Iveson, Lancelot*	1803	Altar Flats, M.S. 17
Iveson, Martha	1810	Altar Flats, M.S. 17
Jackson, Faber*	1681	North Tower, Wa.T. 15
Jackson, George		Lady Chapel, Wa.T. 5
Jackson, Hannah	1700	North Tower, Wa.T. 15
Jackson, Thomas	1706	North Tower, Wa.T. 15
Jowett, Abigail*	1764	Lady Chapel, Wa.T. 23
Jowitt, Frederic*	1846	Sanctuary, S. Side, M.S. 1
Jowitt, John	1860	Sanctuary, S. Side, M.S. 1
Jowitt, Mary Ann	1883	Sanctuary, S. Side, M.S. 1
Kenion, Ann	1760	Nave, M.S. 48
Kenion, Edward	1756	Nave, M.S. 48
Kenion, Elizabeth	1808	Altar Flats, M.S. 27

Kenion, Harriet*	1800	Altar Flats, M.S. 27
Kenion, James	1808	Altar Flats, M.S. 27
Kenion, Mary	1796	Nave, M.S. 48
Kenion, Phoebe*	1747	Nave, M.S. 48
Killerby, Sarah	1824	Nave, M.S. 18
Killingbeck, John*	1715/6	Sanctuary, S. Side, Wa.T. 5
Kilvington, Dorothy*	1803	Lady Chapel, Wa.T. 26
Kirshaw, Anne*	1796	Sanctuary, N. Side, M.S. 1
Kirshaw, Mary	1818	Sanctuary, N. Side, M.S. 2
Kirshaw, Rebecca	1846	Sanctuary, N. Side, M.S. 2
Kirshaw, Samuel*	1786	Sanctuary, S. Side, Wa.T. 7
Kirshaw, Samuel*	1786	Sanctuary, N. Side, M.S. 2
Kitchingman, Elizabeth	1701	Sanctuary, S. Side, Wa.T. 6
Kitchingman, Hannah	1717	Nave, M.S. 21
Kitchingman, Hannah	1723	Nave, M.S. 21
Kitchingman, Hannah?	1811	Nave, M.S. 21
Kitchingman, John	1705	Nave, M.S. 21
Kitchingman, John*	1703	Nave, M.S. 21
Kitchingman, Margaret*	1799	Nave, M.S. 22
Kitchingman, Mary	1770	Nave, M.S. 21
Kitchingman, Thomas	1715	Altar Flats, M.S. 25
Kitchingman, Thomas*	1713	Altar Flats, M.S. 25
Kitson Clark, Edwin*	1943	West End, Wa.T. 1
Kitson Clark, Edwin*	1943	Gallery, Wa.T. 1
Kitson Clark, Ina*	1954	North Aisle, Wa.T. 14
Knowlson, A.		Gallery, Unmounted
Lady Chapel Dedication*		Lady Chapel, Wa.T. 24
Lambertson, Sarah	1785	Altar Flats, M.S. 23
Lambertson, Sarah*	1757	Altar Flats, M.S. 23
Lancaster, Mary*	1826	Altar Flats, M.S. 24
Langton, Agnes	?1464	South Aisle, Wa.T. 2
Langton, ?Agnes	?1464	Nave, M.S. 19
Langton, ?Agnes	?1464	West End, Wa.T. 5
Langton, Eufemia	1465	South Aisle, Wa.T. 1
Langton, Eufemia	1465	Nave, M.S. 20
Langton, Sir John*	1459	South Aisle, Wa.T. 1
Langton, Sir John*	1459	Nave, M.S. 20
Langton, John*	1464	South Aisle, Wa.T. 2
Leathley, Elisabeth*	1778	Altar Flats, M.S. 5
Leathley, John	1803	Altar Flats, M.S. 5
Leeds Pals*		Lady Chapel, Wa.T. 29
Leeds Parish Church A Division*		Gallery, Unmounted
Leeds Rifles*		Lady Chapel, Wa.T. 5
Leigh, Roger Holt*	1831	Lady Chapel, Wa.T. 53
Lever, Anna*	1732	City of Leeds Room, Wa.T. 24
Lloyd, Thomas*	1828	Lady Chapel, Wa.T. 2
Lockwood, Mary	1691	Nave, M.S. 9
Lodge, Ann	1770	City of Leeds Room, Wa.T. 20
Lodge, Ann		Nave Floor, M.S. 63
Lodge, Anna	1754	Nave, M.S. 27
Lodge, Elizabeth	1799	North Tower, Wa.T. 11
Lodge, Elizabeth	1758	City of Leeds Room, Wa.T. 20
Lodge, Elizabeth	1731	City of Leeds Room, Wa.T. 25
Lodge, Elizabeth	1731	Nave, M.S. 63
Lodge, John		Nave, M.S. 63
Lodge, Mary		Nave, M.S. 63
Lodge, Richard		Nave, M.S. 63
Lodge, Richard*	1795	North Tower, Wa.T. 11
Lodge, Richard*	1749	City of Leeds Room, Wa.T. 25
Lodge, Richard*	1656	Nave, M.S. 64
Lodge, Thomas*	1776	City of Leeds Room, Wa.T. 20
Lodge, Thomas*	1710/11	Nave, M.S. 63
Lodge,Henry		Nave, M.S. 63
Lupton, Anna Jane	1888	Gallery, Wa.T. 6
Lupton, Anne	1865	Gallery, Wa.T. 5
Lupton, Arthur	1807	Gallery, Wa.T. 3
Lupton, Arthur	1889	Gallery, Wa.T. 6
Lupton, Charles	1854	Gallery, Wa.T. 5
Lupton, Darnton	1873	Gallery, Wa.T. 5